Counter-narratives of Muslim American Women

Critical Storytelling

VOLUME 6

The titles published in this series are listed at *brill.com/csto*

Counter-narratives of Muslim American Women

Creating Space for MusCrit

By

Noor Ali

BRILL

LEIDEN | BOSTON

All chapters in this book have undergone peer review.

The Library of Congress Cataloging-in-Publication Data is available online at https://catalog.loc.gov

Typeface for the Latin, Greek, and Cyrillic scripts: "Brill". See and download: brill.com/brill-typeface.

ISSN 2590-0099
ISBN 978-90-04-51922-0 (paperback)
ISBN 978-90-04-51923-7 (hardback)
ISBN 978-90-04-51926-8 (e-book)

To Abu, who taught me to be loud and quiet

∴

Contents

Acknowledgments

There is no one who has been more patient with me than Adnan, Maahin, Momin, and Amal. There is strength and love potently packaged right there.

Thank you to Ammi who taught me to dream big and stay small.

My sincerest gratitude goes to the fifteen participants who inspired me with their stories, humbled me with their trust, and opened my eyes to a lived reality that speaks of burden and pride all at once.

This work would not be possible without friends. I'm blessed with truckloads of them, old and new, and I have gnawed at their ears over the last four years. We only remain friends because they are gracious and forgiving of me. I am afraid to name them.

My deepest gratitude to Dr. Corliss Thompson who has mentored me throughout and helped shape my own educational journey. My gratitude also to Dr. Kelly Conn, Dr. Billye Sankofa Waters, Dr. Karen Reiss-Medwed for all the learning and support.

My humble thanks to Laura Meyer and Alessandra Giliberto for all the technical support along the way.

Introduction

The lived experiences of Muslim American youth are situated in a white, mainstream landscape where they traverse their realities as a minoritized and demonized group. The Muslim American population in North America has had traumatizing Islamophobic encounters since the 9/11 attacks, only to be exacerbated further by the hostile bigotry unfurled during the Trump administration. Muslim American youth experience a distinct marginalization experience where they face stereotypes about their religious identity. This lived experience is beset in challenges and resilience, invalidation and courage, as Muslim Americans navigate their intersectional realities with hyphenations and multiplicities of identity at work (Sirin & Fine, 2008).

1   Critical Race Theory and Racialization

While Critical Race Theory (CRT) is primarily deemed a framework that studies racism, the place of religion in human interaction has parallel consequences (Petro, 2017). Racial and religious identities for non-white populations influence the processes and representations of marginalization and othering. Heschel (2015) refers to this as the "slippery nature of racism" through which racism's manifestation is altered while racializing religious identity (p. 3). Grosfoguel (1999) calls this cultural racism, which is prefaced on ethnic absolutism and claims the supremacy of a dominant culture while disparaging all others, while Omi and Winant (2014) suggest that racialization incorporates the "extension of racial meaning to a previously racially unclassified" group (p. 111). Racialization impacts minoritized populations who are perceived as substandard because of their differences from the mainstream. As these differentiating and unique markers are emphasized, a distinguishing identity is created around the particular demographic, featuring unique qualities of "group-ness" that sets them apart from the mainstream (Garner & Selod, 2014, p. 14). Racialization results in the formulation of stereotypes and discriminatory practices which are the primary concerns of CRT (Gerhauser, 2013).

2   Tenets & Application of Critical Race Theory

Critical Race Theory's (CRT) tenets include: (a) the endemic nature of racism; (b) the pertinence of counter-narratives by marginalized people; (c) whiteness

© NOOR ALI, 2022 | DOI:10.1163/9789004519268_001

as norm and property; (d) interest-convergence as a means of initiating change; and (e) challenging neutrality (Lynn & Dixson, 2013). Housee (2012) explicates that in addition to considering macro issues of policymaking, CRT also focuses on "the micro picture of interpersonal behavior, classroom interaction, participation, and related matters" (p. 104). This micro space allows for the conception of counter-narratives that represent the undervalued group's lived reality (Delpit, 1998). An application of CRT includes a challenge to mainstream ideology and propagation of social equity, intercentricity of race and racism, focus on people's experience-based knowledge and application of interdisciplinary methods (Solorzano, 1998). The Muslim American experiential reality benefits from a further exploration through the use of this lens.

The Muslim American experience when explored through a CRT framework can provide keen insight into the unique realities of this demographic. Within scholarship it is critical that we extend beyond Shield's (2004) call of confronting avoidance and silence, and instead craft a new discussion in CRT, that is not only academically theoretical, but one that pivots and engages in an accurate production of counter-narratives of the very people it seeks to study.

Allen (2013) opined that "CRT seeks to challenge dominant claims of race and gender neutrality, objectivity, universalism, ahistoricism, colorblindness, and equal opportunity" because such claims blur the totality of marginalization and "camouflage the self-interests and privileges of dominant groups and maintain the status quo of racial inequalities" (pp. 174–175). Where overt discrimination is clearly observable (Allen, 2013), the covert episodes are prone to be overlooked and go unnoticed. Subtle comments that someone looks good even in a scarf, or that surprisingly one doesn't have an accent, are examples of microaggressions (Sue, 2010). The Muslim experience is plagued with episodes of bigotry and hostility. Acknowledging the experiential knowledge of a marginalized people is one facet of CRT (Tindongan, 2011) and this work seeks to fill that gap in extant literature, by bringing to the forefront narratives of Muslim American youth.

Whiteness makes everything blatantly visible except itself (Leonardo, 2002), and claims to comprehend people's experiences better than they themselves do, extending a deciphering of their worldview and crafting a narrative for them, but without them and despite them (Leonardo, 2002). In addressing inequities and episodes of oppression, whiteness implies that the problem does not exist systemically, or is being rendered an over-sensitized reading, and that BIPOC are fussing over nothing (Crenshaw, 1991; Leonardo, 2002; Sue, 2010). Whiteness pretends to grasp the experience of BIPOC without presenting a space and voice to the oppressed, thereby hijacking and sabotaging their narrative with its own interpretive rendering (Leonardo, 2002). This work crafts that space. It offers the reader an insight into how whiteness interacts with the Muslim American experience through counter-narratives of the demographic itself.

It remains essential that we avoid presuppositions around defining features of ethnic minorities or religious identities because these are often based on multiplicity and varied interpretation. Crenshaw (1995) emphasized that no individual is monolithic, instead they stand at the crossroads of multiple social experiences. Muslim American youth navigate the intersectional reality of multiplicities including the color of skin, heaviness of accent, gender, clothing, countries of origin, and more.

3   Off-shoots of Critical Race Theory

CRT has crafted space under its umbrella for several sub-categories that are particular to different marginalized groups. We see this in the evolution of QueerCrit, AsianCrit, TribalCrit, DisCrit, FemCrit, and LatCrit. Each of these subsets sought to emphasize the unique rendering of oppression to the particular marginalized group in question. The historical development and evolution of these sub-categories of CRT are premised in some essential points:

a.   The experience of marginalization is not identical for all minoritized populations.
b.   Each marginalized population has lived experiences that are particular to them depending on their historical, social, political, cultural, or economic context.
c.   Stereotyping and othering of marginalized people varies in ways specific to them.
d.   The rich intersectional experience of these populations is complex based on the types of hyphenations in occurrence.
e.   Because the experiences of marginalization are specific, CRT, devoid of the application of these micro-perspectives, only offers a broad stroke exploration. These tend to be limiting because of their generic nature and can in turn invalidate, misrepresent, or underrepresent the lived experiences of the very people to whom they seek to give voice.
f.   To craft an authentic space of exploration and understanding it is imperative that a niche is created within CRT that is particular to them and does not utilize the "one size fits all" approach.
g.   Race is a social construct. Racialization is also a social construct. Racism does not limit itself on grounds of pigmentation, but it discriminates across many spectrums wherever marginalization, oppression, or

othering is possible. Racialization of people occurs wherever they can be
herded into a group identity and subsequently othered by supremacists.

4   Racialization of Religious Identity

Despite the evolution of subsets within CRT, a critical micro theory that
explores the marginalization experience of Muslims was not been formulated
yet. CRT blurred the parameters of race in the creation of subsets like QueerCrit,
DisCrit, and FemCrit, however it did not carve a niche for exploring the experience of shared oppression due to religion identity. The Muslim experience
of marginalization ranging from microaggressions to outright bigotry, hostility, and violence were not afforded a distinct subset for exploration within
CRT.

   This work acknowledges that the racialization of Muslims exists regardless of
their "race." Instead, it is positioned around the stereotypical markers of oppressive group-ness. Meer (2012) uncovered "the virtual absence of an established
literature on race and racism in the discussion of Islamophobia" (p. 2) and
recommended we perceive religious bigotry as a racialization. It is therefore
critical to engage in a discourse on racialization by situating it in prevalent conversations of racism (Omi & Winant, 1994). Thomas (2010) suggested that while
one may consider "race as a post-Enlightenment ideology built upon the Atlan-
tic slave trade, hinged upon observable phenotypical human differentiation"
such as pigmentation, physical or biological characteristics; in reality these "dis-
courses of modern racism not only antedate the social taxonomies arising out
of nineteenth-century scientific thought, but it was Christianity which provided
the vocabularies of difference for the Western world" (pp. 1738–1739) thereby
employing religion as the significant indicator of racialization. Thomas's work
recognizes religion as the identifier predating color-based racism.

   Omi and Winant (1994) called religious bigotry a "rehearsal for racial formation" (p. 61); Meer (2012) opined that an investigation of racialization "needs to
commence earlier in order to observe how racialized categories have saturated
cultural portrayals of Muslims" (p. 4). Additionally, Miles (1989) posited that
racialization fabricates "differentiated social collectivities as races" and is a
"nimble meta concept" that should not be reduced to "biological determinism"
(p. 79), but it should focus on social collectives like religion, language, and culture (Meer, 2012). Gans (2016) drew our attention to the fact that racialization of
refugee/immigrant populations should include the lived experiences of people
where the identifiable marker is not purely biological. Racialization "integrates
physical features and social characteristics" wherever a group is "assigned a

new racial identity, interestingly on a social rather than phenotypical basis" (Fassin, 2011, pp. 421–423). Garner and Selod (2014) used the terms "groupness" (p. 14) for this clustering of a social collective. Amrani (2017) elucidated that religion is "raced" when a a population is circled based on characteristics, such as Muslims due to their choice of clothing, name, accent, or country of origin, thereby "reducing an individual to one aspect of their identity" (p. 25). Additionally, Selod (2015) asserted that Muslim Americans are racialized and suffer hostile scrutiny if they have identifiable Muslim signifiers. An examination of racialization indicates that marginalized social groups such as Muslim Americans are categorized as a "race" based on the shared religious association.

5   From CRT to MusCrit

CRT presents us a stage to investigate race relations and power dynamics, while simultaneously impelling the work of social justice forward. A utilization of CRT "moves the center of analysis from individual, to the individual in relation to her political, racialized, environment" (Hernandez, 2016, p. 168) thereby situating the lived experience of the individual in the context of a larger group.

It is pivotal that we craft a niche for the exploration of the Muslim experience as a specific subset in CRT. I refer to this subset as *MusCrit*. The social and political climate is rife with outright hostility and bigotry targeting Muslims Americans. The urgency and intentionality behind coining this term is to create a space within academia that is specific to the Muslim American lived experience. This is a critical step in acknowledging and validating the experiential reality of a people.

6   Tenets of MusCrit

MusCrit provides a micro theoretical framing within CRT that is particular to the experience of Muslim Americans. Key elements from the lived realities of Muslims that necessitate the creation of MusCrit are:

a.   The systemic nature of oppression against Muslims is centered around a white, historical, prejudiced, and monolithic representation of this population. Historically, Muslims have been characterized by the white Christian mainstream as being an anti-democratic, authoritarian, anti-modern, barbaric people. These representations of Muslim have created caricatured and stereotypical identities for Muslims where Arabs are conflated with Muslims, thereby defining all Muslims with a

monolithic essentialism. Mainstream media's current representation of
Muslims feeds into stereotypical narratives of this population. The systemic oppression against Muslims presents itself in micro-oppressions,
extreme violence, policies that are racist and inhibit their movement such
as the Muslim Ban or extreme surveillance, as well as placing the burden
of guilt of 9/11 on every unborn Muslim American. A further implication
of this trend is exhibited in how local Muslim populations are impacted
by foreign policies and affairs. Muslims are not afforded the right to an
individual ethical voice or opinion for fear of being deemed un-Ameri-
can in the process. The US foreign policy in the Middle East influences
the lives of Muslim Americans in ways that no other demographic in a
similar situation would.

b. Identifiability plays a vital role in how Muslims are treated. Women
in hijab (headcover) are more prone to racist attacks and bigotry than
Muslim women who are unidentifiable as such. Muslim men who can be
identified due to their names or beards are susceptible to greater surveillance and threats, and also being perceived as threats, than those who are
not identifiable with religious signifiers. Sikh men suffer hostility because
they are mistaken for Muslims due to their turbans, for instance. Unlike
pigmentation, Muslims may opt in and out of religious identifiability to
protect themselves from racialized threats. Muslims may choose not to
wear a hijab or keep a beard, anglicize their Arabic names, and not pray
or fast in public for the fear of being ostracized. Identifiable Muslims take
on the burdens of micro aggressions and micro invalidations regularly
and are targeted brutally with violence resulting in murder and arson
because of their religious association. When identifiability plays such a
life-altering role in the lived reality of a people, they are compelled into a
double-consciousness due to their hyphenation. Muslims are never considered American enough, or just American, and must always be hyphenated as Muslim-American. They are all required to prove their allegiance
to America and apologize on behalf of the religion for crimes committed
by some few Muslims.

c. Gender performs a crucial role in situating oppressive stereotypes on a
spectrum. Muslim women are often portrayed as oppressed and aggressed
upon by the Muslim men in their lives. Muslim women are therefore considered as controlled and it is perceived that they are not given the freedom
of choice. Their clothing is seen as a symbol of oppression from which they
must be liberated. White savior mentality seeks to free Muslim "captive"
women and assumes that they may not have access to education. Muslim
men are portrayed as oppressive, aggressive, and irrational – who seek to

control and oppress "their" women. Muslim men are demonized and vilified as they are portrayed as terrorists and suicide bombers. Popular media representations of Muslim men in the entertainment industry showcase them as violent.

d. Counter-narratives hold profound significance for a sharing of the Muslim experience. Stories about Muslims are susceptible to getting sabotaged and hijacked by a white telling. In many cases stories about the Muslim experience are untold by Muslims themselves, and in others, voiced over by a white perspective. This leads to an unauthentic and underrepresented rendering of narrative. A white telling of the Muslim narrative portrays them as either oppressed or oppressive. We also notice that literature by (and of) Muslims that gets popularized in the white world is often one that conforms to a white telling. Most college student will have had no exposure to Muslim protagonists in their educational careers except *I am Malala* by Malala Yusufzai and/or *The Kite Runner* by Khalid Hosseini. Both these texts are problematic because these narratives are about a Muslim hero who is portrayed as the exception to the ignorant, barbaric, Muslim mainstream. Additionally, both these books situate the protagonist in faraway Muslim countries (not America), implying that is where all Muslims come from and live. These protagonists are saved by the white world by taking them out of Pakistan and Afghanistan and bringing them to Europe and North America. The mainstream in those barbaric lands were conservative, anti-education, anti-freedom Muslims and the white West had to be the savior in both situations. This generalization of the Muslim experience, reduces and invalidates the very presence of Muslims in America and portrays them as "backward."

e. Whiteness is property and coveted as the norm. Muslims are seen as lacking cultural capital who must be white-washed to become acceptable. Due to prolonged historical encounters with colonization, Muslim population themselves buy into this mindset. Skin-whitening creams, speaking in English, Western clothing, and music are considered superior among Muslim populations in the East and West. Many times, Muslims will choose a self-invalidation of their lived experiences and lack critical group awareness and transparency. Racism against black Muslims by non-black Muslims is embedded in notions of white supremacy that the Muslim population may themselves carry. Muslims may choose neutrality around their own oppression because of these traits of self-invalidation. Muslim immigrants in America often opted to blend into the background, hustle towards the American Dream, silence themselves from making noise, or participate in political and civic spaces as a means of protecting themselves and letting whiteness do its job without comment or question. Muslim immigrants have learned to self-other and see themselves as outsiders even as their children are born and raised here. Being told to "go back home" does not revolt the Muslim consciousness because in many ways they have learned to see themselves as an imposition. While the generation of Muslims who were born in America may read the racial slur "go back home" differently, they are still acutely aware of the favors of the American soil on their parents. The expectation of Muslim representation in literature or movies or history books is slow in the making, because it is seen as benevolence of the White to the unworthy, rather than a right.

f. Essentiality of allies in voicing the injustice against Muslims can be seen in all instances of authentic social-political activism. Discourse on discrimination against Muslims is amplified when other marginalized groups and whites hold the megaphone. Muslim protest against Muslim prejudice does not hold weight on its own as it is seen as irrational or over-sensitized. Despite being a significant minority in the country, Muslim voice is largely ignored unless supported by non-Muslim voices.

7   From Theoretical Framework to Methodology

Utilizing CRT as a methodology enables the creation of counter-narratives by marginalized populations to address the otherwise prevalent deficit and reclaim space (Cook & Dixson, 2013; Solorzano & Yosso, 2002). As a methodology, CRT "generates knowledge by looking to those who have been epistemologically marginalized, silenced, and disempowered" by altering the "margins into places of transformative resistance" as counter-narratives of the marginalized are amplified (Solorzano & Yosso, 2002, pp. 36–37). According to Solorzano and Yosso (2002), counter-stories serve four functions, which include:

1. Community building for the marginalized by offering a human and familiar face to educational theory and practice.
2. Challenging the supposed wisdom of the mainstream by presenting a context to understand and transform established belief systems.
3. Opening windows into the lived reality of the marginalized by displaying possibilities beyond their own and demonstrating that they are not alone in that situation.
4. Teaching others that by melding elements from the story and reality one can build a world that is richer than either the story or the reality alone (p. 36).

Using MusCrit for investigating the lived realities of this marginalized group allows the poignant use of counter-narratives that are indispensable for voice-making. The application of MusCrit as a methodology allows us to capture both how an individual acts and how she is acted upon by the context of her social environment, interactions, and experience (Jones, 2009). Hernandez (2016) asserted that examining identity navigation through such a methodology "for marginalized populations recognizes the increasing complexity of the ways that inequitable social systems may constrain and inform the individual's developing sense of self, and the ways that individuals manage and make meaning out of contextual influences" (p. 168). Through the application of MusCrit, we learn about the lived reality of an oppressed population as they traverse meaning-making of themselves and society. Stories of racialization, discrimination, and resilience, while experiencing a "double consciousness" (DuBois, 1903) or "hyphenation" (Sirin & Fine, 2006) are rendered into a shared retelling.

8   The Use of Narrative Research

A qualitative methodology such as narrative research facilitates a space to gather, retell, and celebrate the stories of the participants (Clandinin & Connelly, 2000). Referred to as counter-narratives within CRT, these stories place the ownership of storytelling with the marginalized population itself (Solorzano & Yosso, 2002). Narrative research is deemed a post-modern methodology upholding the vital purpose of voicing individuals' experiences (Solorzano & Yosso, 2002). According to Clandinin and Connelly (2000), John Dewey's work on experience lies central to the philosophical pretext of this methodology. The researcher takes care to maintain the integrity of the participants' voices and experiences, by generating narrative descriptions that are thick and truly representative of the voice of the tellers. These first-hand accounts of the participants' lived experiences are collected through narrative research, a process in which both the researcher and the participants embark an exploratory journey (Denzin & Lincoln, 2006; Ponterotto, 2005). Chase (2011) described the process of narrative research as "meaning making through the shaping or ordering of experience, a way of understanding one's own or others' actions, of organizing events and objects into a meaningful whole, of connecting and seeing the consequences of actions over a period of time" (p. 421).

Shaping the conversations between the researcher and the participants into thematic and episodic pieces without jeopardizing the voice of the storyteller is the feat of narrative research. This methodology is essentially transformational in nature because it facilitates not only a conversation, but also fosters an empowering experience for the participants in question (Caine et al., 2013). Narrative research boldly provides undivided attention to the lived experiences of people (Clandinin & Connelly, 2000). To be able to achieve this goal, it demands that the researcher and participants share a trust, wherein there is the understanding that the participant is not merely an object of study, but rather a part of the generative process in the creation of poignant narratives (Solorzano & Yosso, 2002). For this study, I maintained an authentic relationship with the participants and was forthright about my own positionality as Muslim American. I executed due attention and diligence in constructing a non-judgmental rapport with the participants so they could share their stories.

Caine et al. (2013) explicated the three-dimensional nature of narrative research of "temporality, sociality, and place" (p. 574) while creating these thematic episodes of storytelling. Chase (2011) situated narrative at the intersections of "biography, history, and society" (p. 421). Tremendous significance is given to the telling and retelling of these experiences to contextualize the juncture in time and place when the events shared occurred. The sharing of stories by the interviewees is in many ways a revisiting and reliving that is being shared with the researcher and being simultaneously interpreted.

Carr's (1986) work on coherence remains elemental to narrative research as thematic episodes are constructed from the participants oral telling. This cohesion renders a process of sharing through learning and reliving of the experience itself. Riessman (2008) growth is at play while this interpretive experience of retelling is at work. For the participants in question, revisiting prior lived experiences allows for memories to take on a more concrete rendering and propel a larger and more engaging conversation.

Narrative research methodology aligned with this project in its goal of creating space through the creation of counter-narratives as it facilitates an "urgency of speaking ... being heard ... the urgency of collective stories, and ... public change" (Chase, 2011, p. 427). This study is situated within an interpretive-critical (Ponterotto, 2005) paradigm as it examines the implications of marginalization on students, thereby providing a call to action for educators, policy-makers and community leaders.

9   The Stories Ahead

The stories shared here speak of the experiences of female, Muslim American students who navigated their formal and informal educational journeys in a country where they are not seen as its own. This book comprises the counter-narratives of 15 female Muslim American students ranging between the ages of 18 and 24. While four of these narratives were collected right after the Trump election, the remaining 11 were conducted after the Biden election. Their stories are different, yet similar, and provide us with rich insight as qualitative data. From seniors in high school to undergraduate college students, these women share intimate narratives of their lived experiences while being Muslim American. Pseudonyms were used throughout this storytelling to maintain confidentiality of the participants. The research employed several hours of individual interviewing conducted either in person or virtually. The questions asked centered around how they navigate their Muslim identity in their daily lived experiences. The presentation of the stories does not follow a chronological sequence, but rather is shared through the creation of thematic episodes. They speak from a place of brave vulnerability, only because they have stories they need the world to hear. They each have a voice that wants to speak its own words.

The participants speak about the impact that their families have had in shaping their identities. They also share the role of the mosque and Sunday religious school in providing them a place of comfort and community. Several participants likewise speak about the role of the Muslim affinity clubs in educational spaces. When talking about peers and colleagues, the participants think about the strengthening of faith and the good relationships it facilitated for them. Several participants had varied experiences of going to a Muslim school for elementary, middle, and/or high school. They thought about the transitioning between religious and secular educational environments and their implications. Additionally, in many instances, the participants explored the impact that participation in extra-curricular activities and opportunities had in their finding a space for themselves. The students shared stories of occupying an uncomfortable spot in predominantly white spaces as well as the comfort and confidence provided to them where diversity was welcomed and celebrated.

As you read these stories, you will learn that identifiability is the key component of living the Muslim American life. Identifiability, as one can imagine, is intrinsically tied to identity itself. While identity may be an internalized experience to some, identifiability grounds that internalized identity in an externalized reality. How one is perceived, how one comes across, and how recognizable one is, is an intrinsic part of the Muslim American experience. This identifiability sets the stage for the racialization of religion and therefore the experiences that follow.

Identifiability in the American landscape is obvious when Muslims pray in public, an act that must be performed five times a day. The second and third prayers of the day fall usually within school hours. Finding a place to pray and then being spotted praying, are all commitments these youth navigate if they are committed to this mandatory act of worship. Non-platonic relationships have many guidelines as well; these translate into no (or very limited) physical contact being permitted between unmarried individuals. This has implications on the social lives of Muslim American students.

Fasting during the month of Ramadhan means these students are not eating or drinking from before sunrise till sunset in that month. Lunch hours can become periods of isolation and also make these students stand out as being the only ones not consuming food. Additionally, there are two major holidays, called Eid, that Muslims celebrate. Because the Muslim calendar is lunar, these dates are not the same each year. Oftentimes predominantly white spaces are unaware of these dates and schedule important events like exams. Vaping, smoking, drinking, and using substances are likewise impermissible in Islam, and Muslim American students may struggle in this regard especially when there is social pressure. Consumption of pork is also not allowed and many Muslims may only eat Zabihah/Halal/Kosher meat which has been slaughtered according to religious prescription. In the absence of these food choices, Muslim Americans often opt for vegetarian or seafood based choices. In school settings this can be difficult to navigate.

Carrying an obviously Muslim name like Muhammad or Akbar can make Muslim American students immediately identifiable. We do see Muslim students taking on different names (giving themselves a Western name), shortening them (like changing Mohammad to Mo), or use anglicized versions of their names (like Joseph to replace Yusuf) to blur the edges of their Muslim identifiability. Muslim males are often also recognized by their beards. Most obviously identifiable is the Muslim woman who is a hijabi (scarf wearing) when she puts on a hijab (headscarf). We see instances of Muslim women obscuring the obvious hijab by styling it in various ways. However, the hijab is very clearly a symbol of the religion and therefore makes them easily identifiable.

A critical part of the counter-narratives shared here is the unanimous experience identifiable Muslim Americans have as they listen to or partake in conversations around terrorist attacks, bombings, shootings, and 9/11. Muslim American youth continue to carry the burden of representing an entire faith on their strong, but young and tired shoulders. Navigating their identities in spaces riddled with stereotypes of demonization and oppression continues to be the experience of Muslim American youth. These stories will help you journey in the shoes of resilient, but repeatedly marginalized youth.

CHAPTER 1

Rahmah's Story

> I'm a minority in America, so I would consider that a big part of my
> identity, because it's something different, and usually, when people
> think about American, they think white American as the standard. I
> just want to specify that and say I'm different – I'm Indian-American.
> RAHMAH

∴

Rahmah is a 19-year-old college sophomore. Born and raised in the Northeast,
her parents were originally from India and had immigrated to the United States
for work. Pursuing neuroscience and physiology, Rahmah is a strong proponent
of women in STEM fields. Rahmah mindfully found ways of keeping her faith
and remained acutely aware of her minoritized presence in the United States.

1   Framing Identity

When asked which terms she would use to define her identity, Rahmah shared
that it would first be centered around race and religion. "I'm an Indian-American.
I'm Muslim" followed by gender, age, and grade. Rahmah's reason for doing this
was:

> I'm a minority in America, so I would consider that a big part of my iden-
> tity, because it's something different, and usually, when people think
> about American, they think white American as the standard. I just want
> to specify that and say I'm different – I'm Indian-American.

Rahmah opined that with increased diversity this thought process was changing, even she first envisions white when she thinks about professors and
professionals and then does a conscious shift in her thinking to make accommodations for non-whites to be American.

While Rahmah makes conscious efforts in expanding her assumptions of
what constitutes American to include herself, she also has to do similar mind

© NOOR ALI, 2022 | DOI:10.1163/9789004519268_002

work in regard to her Muslim identity. "Obviously this is not a Muslim majority country, so I have to kind of implement and remind myself that I am Muslim." When everything around you is not Muslim:

> you have to go out of your way and pray ... stay connected to religion, because nothing around you [facilitates that], like, I don't even go to a Muslim majority college. A lot of my friends tend to lose their religion in college, and I really want to try to keep that.

To preserve her faith "reminding myself and doing things that make me Muslim, because it is part of my *deen* (religion)," requires conscious effort.

Rahmah became involved in the Muslim Student Association to help her engage with other students who desired to connect with faith and had shared needs "like finding a prayer area on campus." Rahmah felt that it was in extra-curricular and non-academic spaces that she could find a niche for her faith, "reaching out to the MSA, going to the Masjid on campus has helped a lot" to maintain her faith which she wants to remain as a "constant."

Through high school and her freshman year in college, Rahmah engaged in different extra-curricular clubs, sometimes because she was interested in them and at other times to just explore different options. Faith "impacted me positively because I didn't think of my religion as like a block for anything ... I didn't think it would bring me down." Rahmah shared that:

> if you stay connected to Islam, you kind of grow and you learn more about it and you learn to love it, so I didn't think of it as an obstacle, I kind of just embraced it and that's why I decided to join the MSA in college, because I knew I wanted to keep that part of my identity.

While faith did not come in her way, "the only negative thing was I didn't have a lot of people to relate to ... and it felt a little lonely at times" revealing that some people who are Muslim have decided not to be engaged with their faith.

Rahmah noticed that not many Muslim students were engaged in the Muslim club in her very diverse high school. Thinking back to that time, she felt that praying and "fasting in Ramadan was a big thing" because at lunch time she would be sitting with her non-Muslim friends and that felt isolating. While she didn't think conformity with the social group was the way to go, she wrestled with the thought:

> oh, just eat something ... it'll be fine if you want to stick with your group ... I tried not to do that, but I was tempted ... it was very difficult but that's the test of patience ... and I kept reminding myself about that.

When you are not among a Muslim majority, hanging on to faith can be lonely work.

2   Finding Friends in Diverse Spaces

Rahmah transitioned from a Muslim elementary and middle school to a public high school and felt that it was "definitely difficult" because she no longer had access to classes that would serve as reminders of her faith. Nobody in high school could relate to the daily practices one does to stay connected to faith except a few close friends that she had had when she was in the Muslim school. "That influenced my choice of friends in freshman year ... I stuck with those people, and they were my main friends in high school."

In college, Rahmah "expanded to more non-Muslim friends ... people who are understanding of why we fast or pray and are open-minded." To scout for these friends, Rahmah would pay attention to their conversations in "religion and history class" to see if they were "open-minded" and see "if they're comfortable about it and also people who had previous knowledge about Islam and stuff, ... like, I knew they would be accepting to something new like this, something new, like me." Rahmah had to "watch out for trends in people" to ascertain if they were "accepting of things," and if they had "certain behaviors." Often times conversations in history class would allow her to "tell from how they speak and how they think about certain human rights issues ... you can kind of see the pattern, and you can see how they think of other people that are different from them." While Rahmah kept her radar out for open-minded people, she also recognized that not everyone knows about Islam, but if they were "willing to learn more about it" or comfortable enough to ask questions, she was always willing to help them learn more.

Rahmah's family raised her as a Muslim Indian American and she was glad that even if she didn't quite understand why her parents said or did certain things, she had reached a point in her life where she agreed with the choices they had made and found them to be right. As an example, she felt it was culturally emphasized that one respects the elders and she now recognizes it to be the right thing. Rahmah felt that a "lot of the things that are in my Indian American culture are very prominent in the Muslim culture and it's basic things that you've probably seen in other cultures, like respect and love and just being a good person," but she also felt there were differences where her ethnic culture may be "conservative" and "patriarchal" when "Islam is clearly not that." The common perception that people have about Islam is that it is male-centered, whereas in reality it maintains gender equity. Many Muslim majority countries in the world may have cultural practices that are patriarchal, but that is not to be conflated with the religion's principles in this regard. All of Rahmah's closest friends are American Muslims and she connects with them because of this shared identity as they "have gone through the same experiences as me." She felt they could:

> understand each other's situation ... we know how their parents are like and this is a specific silly thing, but we know that whenever we try to do something together we know it depends on our parents ... if they are in a good mood or they're in a bad mood ... we understand ... we can text each other and be like, 'guys I can't come tonight' because we all live at home with our parents and we know it depends on what our parents want us to do. If I said that to my white friends, they'd be like 'why are you cancelling last minute,' or 'why can't you just tell your parents.' The threshold of respect in Muslim culture is so different from other cultures.

When Rahmah was in the Muslim school, she was "fine with expressing" that she was Muslim Indian American and everyone around her understood her. Everyone's parents knew each other and she was "comfortable expressing" who she was. Going to a large public high school was a very different experience. "That was when I was trying to not question who I was" but learning "there are other people that were not Muslim Indian-American" which was:

> weird, because I didn't know that there are other people who didn't know who Muslims were at all, which is crazy to me because I remember in freshman year, I told somebody I was Muslim American and they're like I don't know what that is ... and I had thought that Islam was the second most prominent religion in the world ... that you would think that people will know that.

This realization for Rahmah was "not a shock, but it was surprising" that "obviously, white people" did not know.

Rahmah shared that she would be insulted for the Indian food she brought to high school and people would say, "The smell is gross; this looks gross; why are you eating it?" People would negatively question her about her lack of eating during Ramadan. She also shared "in high school I have gotten insulted for my skin color," and she thought of her freshman year when her peers would "compare skin colors on a spectrum" and she would be on the "darker side." Rahmah stated that students engaged in a debate about South and North Indians and that the North Indians "were considered superior because they have lighter skin and I'm South Indian." Rahmah never thought to report any microagressions and would brush it off because she didn't know who to report it to. She never wore Indian clothes to high school "because they are very different from American clothes." Faith guides her family's choice of clothing and they veer towards conservative dressing. "In the summertime all the girls would be in short shorts, and I'd be the only one in long pants and that was definitely very difficult because they had no air conditioning in the high school."

Challenges in high school were part of the growing process for Rahmah who felt that it was fine to be an Indian in her high school since there were many Indian students there, "but to be a Muslim there was definitely harder." She realized while there, "The world does not revolve around me, it revolves around other people." This realization meant that she was not the mainstream or the norm as she had been in the Muslim elementary and middle school. She felt now that was occupying space in a predominantly white world and she was the "other."

Rahmah felt comfortable expressing herself when she went to college. Even though there were not a lot of Muslim Americans on campus, Rahmah felt the diversity in her college included people from all over the world and was very different from her "white, Republican town." She even found joy in being different at college because uniqueness was celebrated with all the international students present there.

3   Experience of Demonization

Each time that 9/11 Remembrance Days took place at high school, where a moment of silence was observed over the high school's PA system, Rahmah "always felt a tension" in the room because people knew she was Muslim. Rahmah shared that:

> everybody would not look at me, but you could tell there's some tension even though I have nothing to do with the 9/11 attacks, but you could still sense that tension … I never looked forward to 9/11 because the energy was definitely awkward and just very uncomfortable … because people know your religion … even though I have nothing, no relation to it.

She further stated that "they would play videos about 9/11 and then they would say 'Muslim terrorists' and this was uncomfortable, because they used those two words together and I was associated with one of those words." Rahmah also thought back to the time of the Boston bombing and how the day right after she bought a huge American flag and put it up in her room. "That was pretty bad because the week after, they found out he was Muslim. I was scared that I was again going to be associated with that word." Rahmah remembers thinking, "I'm also visibly not American, so how is this going to work" and feeling "very awkward and uncomfortable when there was discussion about who did it and why."

Rahmah had gone to sleep the night of the 2016 election and was afraid when she found out the results. Seeing some people in her history class cheer that Trump had won the election scared her. That was the first time she realized her town was republican. "I had never been into politics until then, and as I started researching, I came across things like the Muslim ban." Any time there was a terrorist attack in the world, her first thought was a prayer that the perpetrator was not a Muslim because that would mean the same association again. Rahmah felt that she was definitely perceived as less American because of her religion. She opined that she could change her self-perception to include brown despite the American curriculum teaching students to think of everything through a white mainstream lens. History and the ownership of the country was always placed in white hands and told from that perspective, so it was hard to see how she would ever be considered equally American by others. The only curriculum spaces, where Rahmah ever felt represented, were in history courses when Islam was talked about. Seeing Arabic as an offered course in college felt inclusive to Rahmah.

Breaking the law or going against the rules was unthinkable for Rahmah. She shared that she did not want to disappoint her family in any way or bring them any shame. She shared that her parent's generation came here from India to just live. "They were there to just kind of put their head down and, like, do whatever they wanted and or do whatever was under the law and, just, like, make sure that you're not going out of place or anything." However, she continued, "I don't want to just live, I want to, like, do whatever I want to do … to thrive and make independent choices, and sometimes break the rules if they're not good rules."

CHAPTER 2

Deena's Story

> The essence of being American is being confident in your identity and standing up for what you believe in – that's what every American does.
>
> DEENA

∴

Deena is a 20-year-old studying molecular biology and genetics in New England. Her parents both yield from India but have lived in the Middle East and the United States for parts of their lives. Likewise, Deena has also spent some years of her life in the Middle East.

1   Navigating Identity

When asked to describe her identity, Deena uses the term Muslim American. People usually ask her where she is from to which she responds by informing them that her parents are from India. In "random interactions at stores and with strangers" she feels she is perceived as not being American enough. "When I first meet people and they don't know me yet, they have assumptions that I might not have been born here or that I'm culturally more in tune with a different country." She shared that:

> it had snowed recently and my car was covered with snow and I did not clean the top of it because I was in a hurry to go somewhere. I was at a light and I guess a little bit of the snow and fallen on a car next to me, and he put his window down and started yelling at me saying, 'It's a law here that you need to clean your cars and I don't know if they have laws, where you come from.'

Confident in herself, Deena doesn't feel that she is not American enough. She shared:

© NOOR ALI, 2022 | DOI:10.1163/9789004519268_003

the essence of being American is being confident in your identity and standing up for what you believe in – that's what every American does. I know that a lot of people who were not born here, and maybe moved here in later stages of their life, are not as confident to stand up for things that they believe in, out of fear that maybe they're going to be punished for doing so, especially things like sharing things on social media.

Deena felt that in her daily life being Muslim did not impact her negatively, but she felt "anxiety" and "heightened caution" in the classroom setting because:

I'm a Muslim. People are going to perceive things that I say differently [and] with some inherent biases. So, it's really when I'm in a professional or academic setting that I perceive my own Muslim identity the most and as result of that, I'm a little more cautious of the things I say or the way I behave.

Deena felt that being a brown female, and hijab-wearing Muslim American sometimes gave her an edge where people wanted to increase diversity in their institutions. One of her white colleagues had been rejected from internships, to which another white colleague said she was rejected because she was not a minority group.

Deena had attended a Muslim middle school and felt that impacted her identity as it did for her family members. Her parents remained connected to the mosque, imparted a sense of religious identity, and implemented faith in their daily lives. They taught Deena and her siblings to establish the five daily prayers and that it was never okay to be excused from fasting, even if something conflicted with fasting. Deena's parents taught them to "make your Islamic identity known to other people as well, because Islam is not something that should be practiced in isolation but that it's something that you should be proud of and show to the rest of the world as well." It was during this period of her life and with her mother's encouragement that Deena fully embraced her Muslim identity and started wearing the hijab.

Deena has friends of different religious affiliations, "two Muslim friends, who are like my really, really close friends, and then five who I had met in high school [who are] not Muslim, but they're racially diverse." She shared that her non-Muslim friends have different religions. Continuing she said, "Some of them are atheist and they've mainly shaped who I am because we're all like-minded in the fact that we're all very studious and all very ambitious and driven. We're all very aware of social issues and like to speak up about them." Deena said that "they've impacted my identity. My family shaped my religious identity and my friends have shaped my social identity and how to speak up about my non-religious passions."

Unlike the stories of other Muslim Americans, her transition from a Muslim to public high school was not as difficult as she had thought it would be, largely because she transitioned with some Muslim friends and because the town she lives in is diverse. As a result, Deena did not feel discriminated or bullied in school because of her religion.

2   Treading Carefully

In college, Deena often found herself thinking through what she should share, knowing that her words could be misinterpreted. She shared a story about a time in one of her classes where she was:

> In a slavery and the origins of racism class … and we were talking about the history of white colonialism and white superiority … how before white people discriminated against black people. There was also this sense that if someone wasn't a Christian, they were automatically inferior to you. I wanted to bring up the crusades, but I didn't because … it always happens with me where I'm thinking a thought, and I'm, like, I really want to say it, but, for some reason, it just doesn't come out because I sort of talk myself out of mentioning it, because I'm like everyone's going to think that …

Deena continued to think about this unsurety and also added that when it came to discussing the Muslim-Jewish conflict, she's afraid that "people will think that I'm anti-Semitic or anti-Zionist and I usually just talk myself out of making those comments, even though they might be educational and helpful to mention."

Deena felt largely unrepresented in the mainstream curriculum, other than in Arabic class, and was usually overly cautious about how she was being perceived in classroom discussions. Because Deena had moved from the Middle East to a Muslim school in America, she said:

> It's really interesting because when I moved back to America, I did not know that 9/11 was a thing. My parents apparently did not think that it was important to let me and my brother know that it happened and that the whole world blamed Muslims for it. The first interaction I had with it was at the Islamic school that I went to because we watched a video on it and everyone was very serious that day and I was like what's going on? We

saw a video clip of the plane crashing into the towers and I thought this is
definitely a movie and then later I found out that did happen in real life
and that everyone blamed Muslims about it. Now when conversations
are brought up about it in daily life or on 9/11, I mostly just stay quiet and
I don't say anything about it, it definitely makes me more nervous that I'm
Muslim and that I'm hijabi, and I get all clammy and sweaty, but I usually
just don't say anything.

When any terrorist activity takes place Deena's first thought is:

They're gonna find a way to blame it on Muslims or if it was a white person that it's going to be about mental illness and that nobody brings up
religion unless it's a Muslim – it's not like if Mr. Joe shot a school, they're
not going to be like, 'Oh, he's Christian or Mormon and see how see how
terrible their rules are.'

During high school Deena felt Ramadan always got people curious about
why she wasn't eating. It was not something she bothered to explain or that
drew attention to her. The school's administration would unlock a room for her
to pray in during lunch time. Deena felt that Muslim American males have an
easier time than hijab-wearing Muslim females "unless they have a very clear
Muslim name like Mohammed. Most people can't tell that they're Muslim and
so they might not have certain biases associated with them, [as opposed to] a
hijabi female Muslim."

Deena experiences heightened airport security and every time she travels,
she is pulled to a side for "random checks." She felt that microaggressions often
did not sink in with her unless they were very blatant. She remembered when
on a road trip to Texas they stopped at a gas station and two men looked at her
and said, "Oh my God, look it's a terrorist." She also shared experiences of her
Muslim friends who faced discrimination. Deena went on to speak about how
her Muslim identity caused her to navigate consciously.

Obviously, there's white privilege where you can do anything and get
away with it. I definitely know that I don't have that. I run an activism
account and oftentimes I have to not censor what I'm saying, but be very
careful about what I'm saying, because there's always that fear.

Her personal social media account had been linked to her activism account, but
she had recently disassociated the two because she was "afraid of what people
are going to say." Deena runs the activism account with a friend and they had

posted about crimes against Muslims in France to which they received several hateful comments on their personal pages as well. When they posted about some oppressive incidents, they received comments like "Muslims deserved this" and "your post is massive bullshit; please focus on your own country and stop relaying fake news." After posting on the Uyghur people in China or on the Palestinians, Deena realized that "I need to be careful in terms of my own security and safety."

CHAPTER 3

Hafsa's Story

I wouldn't know how it's like not to be an American because I
haven't lived anywhere else.

HAFSA

∴

Hafsa is a senior at a public high school in a small town in the Northeastern
United States. While her mother and father are both originally from Pakistan,
she was born in Germany, and moved with her family to America in 2001, when
she was less than two years old. Hafsa is the oldest of three siblings, the rest
of whom were born in America. Unlike her younger brothers, Hafsa went to
a private, community-based, not-for-profit Muslim school for her elementary
and middle school years. Upon graduation from a Muslim school, Hafsa transitioned to the public high school of her district. She lives with her parents and
two siblings as a close-knit family.

1 Informal & Formal Educational Experiences

Hafsa's time at the high school was one that moved from an experience of isolation to finding her voice through extra-curricular activities. The role of the
community and mosque were juxtaposed to her early high school experience
of seclusion. Hafsa looked for a sense of belonging in her school, while keeping
a focused lens on her Muslim values and using them to guide her choices. Hafsa
shared stories where she had to make tough decisions to stand up for herself.

2 Difficulty in Transition to High School

The transition from a faith-based elementary and middle school to a public
high school in a predominantly white town proved to be a difficult transition
for Hafsa. She was the only student from her previous school at her new public
school and she spent her freshman and half of her sophomore year being alone.

While her academic focus continued, she was afraid to reach out and make friends, because she was afraid to mix with people who would not hold the same moral values as her:

> I think it was more that the Muslim School is like our whole community, and we all know each other very well. Our parents know each other very well, and we lived with each other since kindergarten. Going from that close-knit community to this high school, where a thousand plus kids are, and everyone has their own little groups, and you can't switch between groups, and you don't know which group is good, which group is bad, which group is more like you. So, that was, I think, the hardest thing.

3   The Strengthening Role of the Community

The mosque played an integral role in providing Hafsa comfort during a time when she was friendless at high school. She still had friends from her previous school and greatly enjoyed going to the mosque and interacting with people from the Muslim community outside of school. This gave her a sense of comfort that even if she was lonely at school, she did have friends elsewhere. The mosque allowed her a space to be spiritually reflective, where she could pray, and ponder upon her good and bad decisions. Hafsa mused that the mosque was a place "where I felt closest to being whole."

Hafsa found a group of like-minded people in the Robotics club at her high school. She shared that the reason why she got along so easily with everyone on the team was because it was very diverse; in fact there was a joke on campus that "all the colored kids flock to the Robotics team." About segregation on color lines, Hafsa sensed "all the white kids tend to hang out with each other anyways, and then you have our group of Asians with the occasional white person" who gravitated towards Robotics because they were "the top of their class" and motivated academically. The diversity in the Robotics team was not representative of the school itself, which has a predominantly white population. According to Hafsa, the students on the Robotics team all exhibited the same kind of values and understood her better. Hafsa felt she wouldn't have been as "social, loud, and techy" as she was, had she not been on the Robotics team.

> A lot of them share the same values as me, which I'm really glad of, that I found people like that because I didn't want to have to either change mine or find others or change them, or not even be with people for the rest of the high school.

Hafsa stated that her choice of sports was restricted due to the clothing norm at school. She shared that when she did track at school, the meet uniform caught her by surprise, because she wasn't expecting it to be comprised of shorts and a tank top. She was told that not being in uniform would not allow her time to counted. Finally, she worked out a solution where she wore full length spandex leggings and a full-sleeve shirt under her track uniform to be able to participate.

Her values and choice in clothing differed from the mainstream. Hafsa explained how clothing choices were "second nature" to her, and while she might consider the clothes of those girls pretty, she certainly didn't feel the desire to wear them, "I'm not gonna walk around in shorts at school because it just feels wrong ... It's not something that I want to do, and it's not something that I do."

4   The Role of Parents and Acculturation

Hafsa's parents were deeply committed to the academic achievement of their child and provided her with support and motivation. She felt that her mother was largely unaware of the socialization challenges at school and could not have helped Hafsa adjust better in her beginning years in high school. Hafsa also cited an example about her parents' differing viewpoints. One evening as her mother came to pick her up, she saw Hafsa standing alone talking to a male teammate. Her mother cross-questioned her intensely about who he was and what they were talking about. The next day her father came to pick her up. That evening she was also standing alone talking to another male team-mate. Her father didn't notice this as odd and did not question her at all. Hafsa reflected that they varied in their understanding of socialization norms. "I think my Dad, since he works in such a diverse work environment, he under-stands that there shouldn't be a physical barrier between you two, that you can talk and not have anything going on."

5   Defining American and Intersectionality

When Hafsa traveled to Pakistan recently it allowed her insight into what made her American. Her visit was comprised of two locations, a cosmopolitan urban city, Lahore, and a suburban traditional city, Sheikhupura. Hafsa felt that in Sheikhupura "they all just really stared at me, so I didn't like it that much." On introspection, she discovered parts of her that were very distinctly American. In Pakistan, women generally do not drive a motorbike, and when they do ride one as a passenger, the cultural norm is that they sit sidesaddle with both legs on one side of the vehicle. When Hafsa sat with her legs straddling the seat, her uncle said, "Wow, this really makes you look American, just sitting like that in that way." She also felt that people would stare at her there if she wore "American clothes like sweatpants" so she made sure to only pack Shalwar Kameez when she traveled to Pakistan. Hafsa felt there was judgement about her not being able to cook, or not being interested in clothes that other Pakistani girls were interested in there. Most interestingly, Hafsa felt an American aspect of her personality was being able to fix gadgets that other girls in Pakistan would not attempt. She felt empowered as an American girl to be able to do this.

6   Connection to Curriculum

Hafsa could not recollect a time when she found herself specifically represented in the curriculum. During a class on European History, she chose to do a presentation on Muslim contributions and found representation in that activity. In the character of Atticus from *To Kill a Mockingbird*, she found a character who, like her, stood for his beliefs. Hafsa joked about *The Handmaid's Tale*, and how the character made a "big stink" about wearing long robes and covering herself, whereas Muslim women do it without that concern.

7   Interactions with Teachers and Microaggressions

During gym class, Hafsa had an interaction with her gym teacher, a "very very white" teacher, who said to her, "Oh, you're a Muslim, I thought you were supposed to be shy and all that," to which Hafsa responded "that's like saying all Christians should be the ones who go to church and act really nice to everyone, and I don't see you doing that." When asked to describe what Hafsa meant by the teacher being "very, very white" she explained that these were people she was sure were Republican.

> In our school, if you describe someone as basic white, you're talking about the rich, the white, the Christian, the WASPs. Someone taught me this acronym once, and I like to use it a lot … he was a total WASP, and he was also very strong about his beliefs.

Other than this one interaction, Hafsa felt her overall high school experience with instructors had been clear of discriminatory speech.

CHAPTER 4

Rania's Story

Maybe some exchanges might be easier if I wasn't wearing hijab, like people wouldn't get nervous when they first saw me.

RANIA

∴

Rania is an 18-year-old college sophomore studying chemistry in New England. Her parents originate from India and she has Muslim and Hindu relatives. Rania loves learning and hearing people's stories. Rania describes herself as Muslim Indian American and shares that, while she has Indian heritage, she wasn't born there. Media and people around her perceive her as less American and are "shocked when they realize I was born here. I've been told my English is so good and I say to them, yeah, I was born and raised here so my English is going to be pretty decent." Rania shared that in one of her college classes her teacher called her out in class and said, "You weren't born here, right? Can you tell us a little bit about your immigration story?" Rania said that she doesn't mind explaining because people "don't really mean to hurt us." Regardless of how she is perceived, Rania considers herself to be American enough because:

> being American is being different and being open to different opportunities, different views, and America is a land of diversity, it's a land of immigrants and just because some people don't view it that way doesn't take away from the fact that that is what American is.

1   Hijab & Identity

Rania felt that her identity impacted her daily life in the language she spoke, her interactions with her relatives, her food, and the acts of faith that she performs. Wearing the hijab impacts her presence in the world because if she didn't wear it, at:

first glance people would not know I was Muslim. I would like to think that I would still tell people I was Muslim if they asked … I wouldn't try to hide it, but I would definitely not be asked as many questions as I am. Maybe some exchanges might be easier if I wasn't wearing hijab, like people wouldn't get nervous when they first saw me.

Rania started wearing the hijab in 7th grade and recalls being very excited about putting it on and didn't really realize how difficult it would be until I got to high school." Hijab makes it difficult "to make friends at first sight. You're always very nervous; you think am I going to get picked last for everything … and people who don't know you start associating [you] with what they've seen on TV." Rania felt that she had to make more deliberate attempts at making connections with people as they "just kind of undermine you a lot. They don't tend to ask your opinion and you have to make more of an effort to stand out or to prove yourself."

Rania has engaged in different volunteer opportunities and clubs in her high school and college and felt that she resonated with groups that were minoritized as well, such as the Black History or Asian clubs. She said her reasons for joining these clubs were to connect with other people who shared her identity or were open to diversity. Rania shared that "it may seem pretty restricting" to lead her life as a Muslim American because "you have to try to fit in your prayer time like according to your schedule." While that may be difficult, it:

> also opens up opportunities to be an ambassador for Islam, you can talk about your experiences, people will ask you questions, and it feels good that you do get to portray Islam in a positive way and correct the misconceptions that people may be holding.

2   Influences on Identity

Rania shared that her parents have had a deep impact on her identity and the practice of her faith. They encouraged her to pray with reminders and would discuss religious topics and the Friday sermon. She felt these conversations helped shape her identity and clarified misconceptions. When Rania travels to India, she feels that her relatives there perceive her as very Western because of her clothes and accent. Rania also feels that the adults in the Muslim community in America are judgmental and keep tabs on what Muslim kids do and then talk about it. She believes that can add pressure on those youth and push them away from Islam. Her belief is that the communities "should be there to

uphold you and strengthen you; but sometimes they mix up culture and religion and then judge people for their mistakes which pushes them farther and
farther away."

Conversely, Rania sensed that some of her peers probably judged her for
being too Muslim because she wore the hijab. She was often asked by non-
Muslim peers why she wore the headscarf when other Muslim girls didn't, but
"that would be a difficult question for me to answer because I can't put others
down, because wearing the hijab doesn't necessarily put me on a higher level,
so that's always hard to explain." Rania also felt that the Muslim community was
always very happy when someone converted to Islam, but they were never really
there to support the converts on new their journey. But for Rania, she shared
that the friends closest to her were Muslim which "helps to keep faith intact"
because they remind each other to pray. "You have others standing with you
and they go through the same struggles with you and understand what it's like."

3   Uncomfortable Interactions

Rania started feeling the differences in her identity in high school and not
before that. In her college class recently, she was called upon "out of the blue to
talk about the hijab." Rania shared that she would have prepared if the teacher
had emailed about it beforehand, but instead she was caught off guard to
speak about her hijab to a mostly white class. At times, she "feel[s] sometimes
people expect you to explain yourself, even when that's not really your job; you
shouldn't be expected to do that." Rania did not find herself represented in the
curriculum and didn't recall ever learning about people like herself in public
school. Her classroom experience showcased that "I've kind of had to wait for
a turn to speak, but once I do start speaking, people are willing to listen, and
they understand that I do have things to say." She feels "nervous and awkward"
when people talk about 9/11, because it feels like "everyone's staring at me and
you know, I wasn't even born at that time; it's unsettling that people keep associating it with all Muslims." Anytime there is a terrorist attack or a shooting,
Rania's first thought is that she is afraid it will be a Muslim who did it. "It's
sad, but when you watch the news and find out it's not a Muslim, you relax"
because if it is a Muslim:

> everyone's gonna be talking about it, but with a white person the conver-
> sation doesn't last too long, after a few days you will forget about it. But
> if it's a Muslim, everyone keeps talking about it for weeks, that this act of
> terrorism has affected our country.

She shared when teachers discuss it in the classroom, it is "awkward just sitting there, even though you know you have nothing to do with it, but this is connecting your identity to that because they connect identity to those cases as in its Muslim terrorists so I feel that impact." Rania continued to emphasize that Muslims have nothing to do with this, but stereotypes about Middle Eastern Muslim terrorists exist, and even some of her liberal friends had told her that their parents "view Muslims in a negative way. Even though they don't associate them with terrorism, they still think Islam is not like a good religion."

Rania found her college to be predominantly white and has not come across any other student yet via Zoom in her classes who wears a hijab. She felt that diverse spaces felt more welcoming to students of color. She remembered in a club meeting, several white and some non-Muslim Indian students started making fun of Islam and how around Eid, Muslims sacrificed animals by shouting, "Allahu Akbar" to each other. This really hit her hard, and she shared, "I was in my early years of high school; I was not super confident yet and I didn't really like to address people I didn't know." Even though she felt anger, she did not say anything at that point. She felt other Muslim students in her high school:

> feared being found out that they were Muslim; they tried to hide the fact that they're Muslim and that was a very common thing, so I think they [are] kind of like ... you are afraid of that happening before it even happened.

These other students would "avoid the subject," wouldn't "tell others they were Muslim," and try not to engage in social media posts that were pro-Muslim "because they didn't want anyone to find out." Regardless of what she encounters, the hijab is an important part of Rania's identity and she does not feel fear in wearing it in public.

CHAPTER 5

Mehar's Story

> A very, very big part of why I do what I do and am who I am today is
> because of moving to America.
>
> MEHAR

∴

Mehar's family moved from Iraq when she was six years old. She now lives
in the Midwest and is studying neuroscience and psychology. Her father used
to work for an American business in Iraq, and after some threats were made
against their family in Iraq, "they got him special immigrant visas for his family" to move to the United States. Mehar described herself as an "Iraqi American, first generation student, and a hijabi." Mehar felt "that a very, very big
part of why I do what I do and am who I am today is because of moving to
America" and this was possible because of the sacrifices her parents made in
leaving their home and family in Iraq behind, so that the children could be
safe and have a good education. This pushed Mehar to remain "academically
focused." Mehar grew up in a Shia household, and while her family gave her a
basic grounding in faith, teaching her to pray and taking her to Sunday School,
they otherwise took a backseat when it came to religion.

1   Relationship with Her Hijab

Mehar started wearing the hijab when she was nine. Talking about the hijab,
she shared, "Obviously, the hijab has been a big thing in my life." One of her
elder sisters had taken the hijab off and another one had taken it off in high
school, but then put it back on. Mehar recalled that their choices of taking it
off were related to questioning their faith, if there was reason to wear it, if they
didn't agree with it, or to just look pretty without it:

> I always kept it on, but that experience has always made me think about
> the hijab. In college too, there are a lot of Muslim girls who don't wear it
> or wear it in a different way, so it's always been something that I've had to

answer for myself and I think the answer has changed over the years. And then there's obviously politics ... I grew up in a very white town and I was the only Muslim American going to high school. It didn't make me feel different. I adjusted fine, but that was always a very, very big part of my identity because there was no one else around who was Muslim.

Mehar thought about how her perceptions have changed over the years. "When I first put it on, it was a very exciting thing and I did it to follow in my sister's footsteps. I liked wearing it; my mom, more like my whole family, wore it." As Mehar transitioned to high school she said:

> I started thinking why I wore it and my reason then was I just didn't like the way my hair looked. I liked its style and I didn't even question it and going into college, I really grew into it. And I love wearing it now because I love being a Muslim.

Mehar found her college environment to be "very welcoming and accepting of it, so I can very proudly be Muslim and love the culture it brings with it."

2   Sense of Community

Mehar has been involved in extra-curricular activities during her educational journey. From being involved in academic competitions, to starting a diversity club, to being in the Muslim Student Association and other BIPOC groups, Mehar has a wide range of interests. She enjoys going to Middle Eastern and Pakistani events and loves having the sense of community being among Muslim students gives her. Because she is "proudly Muslim American," her participation in fun events planned by the MSA brings her joy, "but at the same time, there are things that I don't see myself joining as a Muslim American like sororities." Mehar frequented the mosque when she was younger and went to Sunday School:

> When I was a kid, I don't think I appreciated them or never wanted to go to Sunday school, but now realizing that I had face to face interaction with very, very intelligent and qualified religious leaders, I kind of regret not paying attention.

Mehar's closest friends at college were those girls she bonded with over religious or cultural similarities. When making friends, Mehar sought to see people who could acknowledge her Arab/Muslim identity, who would be comfortable enough with her sense of humor centered around her identity, show some "lack of ignorance," and know that Muslims pray and don't wear the hijab in the shower! If people approached Mehar with a conversation, she saw it as a sign of someone being open. When Mehar sees groups that are all white, it signals to her that she is not welcomed there.

3 Questions of Identity

Mehar felt that she may come across as not being Muslim or Arab enough to the Muslim community and not white enough to the mainstream in America. She felt a lot of that had to do with the hijab which made her "visibly Muslim" and may make other people feel that she was not approachable. Mehar thought that a lot of her humor came from her identity of being Muslim American and "white kids" would not be able to relate to that experience. Mehar considered herself to be "much more American than Iraqi." In fact she found herself to be "too American" when she had last traveled to Iraq. Within the Muslim community, Mehar felt there were some who would consider her too Muslim, and others who would consider her not Muslim enough. "I think it's ridiculous; I think it's wild, especially considering the range of experiences that Muslim Americans have whether they're immigrants, second generation, or third." To Mehar the religious journey was a personal one and not one that asked for judgement. She spoke highly of a Muslim mentor at her college whose work was making the MSA an inclusive space that wouldn't emphasize on being judgmental. While Mehar did not consider herself to be Iraqi enough, she was satisfied with her relationship to her faith.

4 Early Experiences in America

Mehar reminisced how in elementary school her focus was to:

> learn English, figure out how to make friends in America, understand the culture – a lot of that was like a crash course in being American, and I think a lot of immigrant kids ended up predominantly speaking English at home, like in the beginning I was so immersed in it and excited about it.

Mehar also thought back to being in fourth grade and fasting during Ramadan. "Not being in the cafeteria, going to the library and reading because I didn't want to be with students eating ... it made me feel very special and empowered as a kid." She remembered all her friends being white in elementary school. She recalled:

There are a lot of times, where I knew deep inside that I didn't relate to these kids and they were probably not the best influence on me, but because schools were so small, I just kind of rolled along with it because I'd rather have bad friends, than no friends. I definitely tried to fit in in every single way, except taking of my hijab. I got bullied for my clothes, and kids would ask me why I was wearing what I wore, and then I switched to jeans and hoodies to emulate what I saw. I remember really wanting to get a phone because everyone had a phone and my parents were very strict Muslims and said 'you don't need a phone.'

Mehar also shared that she had a unibrow growing up:

I hated my unibrow and I took a scissors and cut [it] off. My mother didn't say anything which was really nice of her. Kids would point out my unibrow, point out the kind of things that made me Arab, and made me very insecure, in middle school, especially.

Her middle school experience was slightly diverse and she met more immigrant students, but the "teachers saw me as different because I was in a hijab." Mehar pointed out that she did have some good teacher mentors along the way. In high school she shared that her faith "got definitely worse." She hung out with non-diverse friends only because it was better than not having friends at all. Mehar shared:

every time we hung out it was stereotypically American things like board game nights and taco night but with no flavor. I just kind of put up with it and I tricked myself into thinking, I was having fun, but I wasn't. I never got into like partying like that side of high school.

As far as some extracurricular activities, she felt that her sports choices were very limited because they were not friendly to the clothing choices she had to make. She felt she didn't learn to swim because of clothing limitations and skipped homecoming because she couldn't find a dress that worked.

5   Uncomfortable Interactions

Mehar could not find herself represented in curriculum except when the Ottomon Empire may have been discussed. She felt that when the Middle East was discussed in class, there was an unsaid expectation that she would have something to say about it. When asked how conversations about 9/11 made her feel, she responded, "Oh man, usually I'm disappointed with the little amount of information that I hear in these conversations." Mehar also felt that 9/11 was attached to several events on the Muslim world. Terrorism in countries like Yemen, Iraq, and Syria were seen more through a lens of there being attacks on the United States, than how the people of those countries were suffering. When any terrorist attack takes place globally, Mehar's first hope is that the person who committed it is not Muslim:

> I definitely remember Charlie Hebdo happening, and I remember my dad and me posting on social media, 'I am Charlie Hebdo' and it made sense to me then ... but look[ing] back I'm annoyed that I have to do this every time that there's a shooting.

Mehar understood that attacks of these nature were big things, but there was also this expectation of her to post public condemnation because she was Muslim.

In her high school years, Mehar faced microaggressions like being stared at and laughed at, or by people loudly making pro-guns and pro-Trump comments when she was around. Sometimes at night, when she was passing by, she felt unsafe because of her hijab. "Some guys were screaming salaam or things about blowing up – those were times when I've been genuinely afraid." She also recalled a hijabi friend being assaulted and yelled at. These experiences of overt oppression and micro-aggressions are intended to intimidate and watching out for intimidation, gauging where to place threats on a spectrum of severity is a normalized experience that this population has to mal-adjust to quite often.

CHAPTER 6

Amber's Story

> I think the fact that I have such light skin and the fact that I don't
> wear a hijab is what's kept me from ever experiencing outright dis-
> crimination.
>
> AMBER

∵

Amber goes to large diverse public high school in a growing small town in suburban Massachusetts. Prior to high school, Amber went to a faith-based, community run Muslim school for her elementary and middle school. While Amber was born and raised in Massachusetts, both her parents originally come from Morocco.

Amber shared stories of engagement and involvement in many different activities, which not only eased her transition to high school, but also defined her personality and attitude. Amber's struggles with identity were minimal as she navigated her social spaces with ease. The role of the mosque and community offered her comfort as did knowing that in a diverse world she was not much different than others around her. Amber took decisions of finding herself with choices of integration and assimilation over her high school years.

1   Defining Self, Race, and Ethnicity

In a recent activity during her Human Geography class, Amber was given the task to pick 10 words that identified her. Her original list included words like student, sister, pole vaulter, Muslim, Moroccan, American, and more. By the end of the activity, the students were asked to engage in conversation with their peers and strike out one identifier at a time. For Amber, the final remaining word was Moroccan. She felt that between the terms Muslim and Moroccan, when asked to give up one, she gave up Muslim, knowing that being Moroccan came with the assumption that one was most probably Muslim as well, whereas if she picked Muslim, it would not capture her ethnicity at all.

© NOOR ALI, 2022 | DOI:10.1163/9789004519268_007

Ideally, she would have wanted to say Moroccan American, but for the activity that was an invalid choice. She shared:

> When you think American like in the sense of today what an American is, it can mean anything. It's such a broad range. I feel like if I say Moroccan, people understand my background a little bit better than just throwing myself into a melting pot.

Amber explained that the Moroccan aspect of her was what made her unique from most people around her. She identified her features, the food she ate, and her ability to speak the native Arabic dialect, even if she struggled to read and write in it as being distinctly Moroccan. When questioned if she had been asked to do the same activity on identity in a Moroccan high school, where everyone else around her shared that aspect of ethnicity, she reflected that her remaining identifier in that geographical setting would have then been American instead:

> If I were in Morocco, then everyone there would already understand the connections to the word Moroccan. In America, it has a totally different meaning. People see it as a foreign word, but it defines who I am. If I was already there and everybody identifies the same way, I feel like if I was doing an activity where I wanted to show other people more about me, I would probably pick American.

Later, Amber mused, if she was in a third geographical location, she would go with Moroccan, and if allowed to pick a double identifier she would go with Moroccan American. Being unique therefore, was the most significant marker of identity for Amber. Race and ethnicity held clearly different meanings for Amber, one as something that others identified you based on how they perceived you physically, and the other as a self-identifier. Amber reflected "race doesn't really exist" when asked to identify her race, however her ethnicity was very clearly Moroccan, but her identity was Moroccan American.

2   Finding Strength in Diversity

Overall, Amber did not feel that her identity as a Muslim American impacted her life in any significant way sharing, "I'm not doing anything that would require it to play a huge role in my life. I usually go to school, come home, go to work/robotics." Amber mentioned how when faced with food choices, she steered clear of eating pork, but there were other meat and vegetarian options

that were always available for her to choose from. Being a part of her high
school was easy because Amber found it to be very "inclusive." About her track
team Amber mentioned:

> There are a lot of Muslims on the track team. It's great because there
> are the people that wear their Hijabs and the Under Armor (referring
> to the complete leggings and full-sleeved attire under the sports team
> attire), but there's also people that will wear shorts and tank tops. They
> all identify as Muslim, and we interact all the time. It's really interesting
> to see because there's not many places where you'll see such a mixture of
> people.

Amber felt that her high school was diverse in that it had many students of
color, primarily including people for Southern and East Asia. She stated that
her high school supported students "being true to their faith" and celebrated
uniqueness in students. The Muslim Student Club at the high school had several participating students. According to Amber, the Muslim students in school
were mostly identifiable, not always because they chose to wear the scarf, but
because the school culture was okay with people being different. Amber mentioned many other Muslim students on her Robotics team and how everyone
knew they were Muslim because of their food choices which always came up
when the team ate together. Amber felt that because there were also many
Hindu teammates, the coaches were very mindful of making sure that the
menu on meeting days was inclusive. Amber reflected:

> We have such a mix of people of different faiths and different ethnicities
> that there's always someone there that doesn't fit the general majority,
> and so even if you do feel different, there's always other people that are
> doing their own thing too. So, you never feel completely alone.

3   Parents and Acculturation

Amber felt that her parents' greatest role in her identity formation was in that
they chose to send her to the Muslim school, and how that made it possible
for her to engage in all the extra-curricular activities that she was a part of.
Additionally, Amber thought that her parents made a concerted effort to pass
on the Moroccan heritage to her. She shared:

> They raised me speaking Arabic, so it was my first language and I spoke
> it better than English until a large part of my younger childhood … and

they do take us back to visit Morocco, so they have played a large role in keeping me connected with my heritage and my Muslim roots.

Additionally, when Amber first began high school, her mother would often remind her of the years of learning at the Muslim school and that Amber should keep those values as guiding principles through high school. Regardless of the advice her mother gave her, Amber explained that her parents had not hindered her. "They've let me ... throughout my four years of high school ... they've given me advice and what not, but it's been on me to figure out who I am."

4   Values

Amber felt that she had been very lucky in the friends she made during her freshman year as they did not partake in drugs or wild parties. "In the times that it has come up with other people, like friends in different classes or people on the robotics team, I have avoided things like that because of my religion."

The experience of buying a dress for prom was not very difficult for Amber. While she was not looking for something long-sleeved, she did want "something that was closed for the most part. I definitely didn't want a leg slit or something like that, or a completely open back or low cleavage." She felt there were plenty of options to choose from in that range and knew of people who got their dresses altered for modesty by adding mesh or length. She said there were Muslim girls who went for dresses that covered more and everyone was understanding of their choices. While Amber did go to prom with a boy, she felt it was okay because they were all part of a Robotics group. Amber loved dancing at the prom and recalled how she got in trouble at the Muslim school for dancing around in fourth grade, where her teacher called her mother to report the "inappropriate behavior."

Amber felt that being Muslim American did affect parts of her life, "but when I'm in school learning, it doesn't change or it doesn't make me any different from the person sitting right next to me." Coming from the Muslim school, one of the adjustments that Amber had to make was getting used to seeing couples walking in the hallways. This was weird for Amber, coming from an environment that had been heavily gender segregated. Amber felt at the Muslim school, there was great emphasis on seating boys and girls separately, but in high school they were assigned projects together. She soon realized that all students worked together and hung out together despite the gender. She concluded:

I think that once you leave a sheltered place like the Muslim school and you're brought into, whether it be high school or college, it's now on you to develop your own idea of the world. You can't constantly have the same ideas that people have been telling you your whole life. So, once you get past a point, people have given you as much information and guidance as they can, but you reach a point where you have to make your own decisions and your own judgments based on what you yourself feel.

CHAPTER 7

Selma's Story

> I'm so ready to represent the Muslim Ummah in a way that I know others have done before me, but I want to hop on that bandwagon as well.
>
> SELMA

∴

Selma described herself as a Muslim American while also being Palestinian and Syrian. Her mother was well grounded in faith, a Palestinian, born and raised in America, whereas her father was a Syrian immigrant, and liberal in his practice of faith. Having parents from diverse backgrounds and levels of religiosity gave Selma a unique experience at home. Selma went to a Muslim school from third grade all the way through high school along with her younger brother and sister, whereas her older brother remained at public school throughout his education.

1   School

Selma transferred to the faith-based school in third grade from the public school system, because her mother wanted to give the children an Islamic education. Selma struggled with subjects like Arabic, Quran, and Islamic Studies that she had not studied formally prior, and felt that other students, who started the school earlier than she did, had a better grasp of the academics even in the later years.

For Selma adjusting to her new school was easy socially. Recalling back to third grade Selma said:

> Making friends was interesting because I didn't have girls in my class named Jessica or Lauren or Kelly. I had girls named Maham and Fatima and Rahma, and I was like, 'Okay, this is different, but I can make friends with you; my name is Selma, and you guys can pronounce my name right, not like the girls in my public school.'

© NOOR ALI, 2022 | DOI:10.1163/9789004519268_008

2   Transitioning to College

Selma recalled experiencing anxiety about her transition to college. She was cognizant of the challenges that might face her when she moved to college, because this would be her first step away from the comfort zone of a community school. One of her criteria in making the choice of college was based on how diverse the school would be. She shared a time when she had talked to someone about transitioning to college and they told her, "You have to be very careful as a Muslim American surviving" because she had a disadvantage and may be walked over. She continued:

> When she told me it's a disadvantage, I was like, wow, that's very hard … because she was like, 'That's why a lot of girls take off the scarf, and that's why a lot of girls don't want to identify as that, or they change their name from Jannah to Jen, because they don't want to have that Muslim identity.' When that girl told me it's kind of a disadvantage, I was like, actually I kinda think it's my advantage because I'm different, I'm unique, and although there are 1.7 billion Muslims in the world, most Muslims are being labeled as something they're not, and I'm gonna prove people wrong. I want to represent my Muslim Ummah in the best way possible.

Selma is hopeful that she will maintain her faith and keep her strong sense of identity through college. Yet at the same time, she was very nervous about some things she had heard from her friends about Muslim girls, with similar backgrounds as hers, who had gone to college and soon decided to take their hijabs off, partied hard, and drifted away from their values. She said, "Now, I'm very strong within my deen (faith). I couldn't be happier, and I know that in college it's going to be tough, but I hope, inshallah, I remain so intact with the scarf." Selma prays that she will remain strong.

She was also scared about being in New York among diverse people, if there was another extremist attack and the perpetrator was Muslim. She was afraid that people would judge her on the streets and be afraid of her because of her hijab. Selma was prepared to speak on behalf of the Muslim Ummah, if there were people making Islamophobic comments. "I'm just a Muslim girl trying to survive, basically, in this country, and to represent my Ummah well and educate myself."

3   Choosing to Wear the Hijab

For Selma, the decision to wear the hijab a year and half ago during high school was a very conscious decision that she wanted to make before she went off to college. Her friends considered her religious because of this choice, and while Selma was proud of her decision to wear the scarf, she was also humble about how a physical scarf was not enough of a marker of one's religious practice. She elaborated:

> You can wear the scarf, but if you're not making your prayers on time if you're not doing good deeds, if you're not giving charity, if you're not doing X, Y, and Z, what we're supposed to do as Muslims what does the scarf really matter? It's just a veil.

In her journey she consistently questioned her intentionality. She reflected on her decision to wear the hijab:

> I was going into 11th grade I was like, you know what I want to put it on. I had toxic people in my life at that time, and I felt like I was doing it just to impress a particular person or impress all my friends.

As a Muslim, it was important that she not do it to show off to people, but that she wears the scarf from her heart and purely for the sake of pleasing God. To this end, she rethought her decision a few times, taking it on and then taking it off, wearing it for making an impression on people, to finally doing it because of her recognition of it being a command of God. She remembered being exasperated with herself as she oscillated between different emotions about wearing the hijab, wondering if her heart was in it or not, doubting herself, wanting to take it off, and thinking what people would say, to finally at one point it just clicked with her:

> I was like, yo, my heart is in this forever. I'm like, and I hope it stays in my heart forever, because I love the scarf, I love what it identifies me as like a strong, powerful Muslim woman. This scarf that I'm wearing, ancestors before me have worn this scarf like some of the most influential women in Islamic history have worn this scarf, I want to wear it.

In her own experience, Selma felt that she has experienced more Islamophobia ever since she had started wearing the hijab. Before she wore it, she felt she could pass off as white and not a Muslim, because she was light-skinned and unidentifiable as Muslim. Selma reflected that she knew how life was when she did not wear the scarf, and how the perception about her in people differed because of her choice of covering when she did start wearing it:

I know the difference right away because when I used to not wear the scarf, I would be treated like, 'Hey, what's up,' from anyone. I would get smiles from strangers because they wouldn't know that I'm a Muslim. They wouldn't know that I'm Arab, because I'm not wearing a scarf [and] my hair is down. But [when] I wear the scarf, it's a completely different situation. When I used to not wear the scarf, I would be a light-skinned girl with whatever color my hair is, and I would walk around, go on the beach, go on the boardwalk, and everyone would treat me, 'Hi, hey, what's up.' I would get a slice of pizza and the guy wouldn't look at me like I was like, 'What, wait, you speak English?' It's so crazy because when you wear the scarf, and you talk in English to a person that's American, just look at their face, because they look at you and they're like, 'Oh my god, they can speak English.'

Wearing the scarf is a symbol of her faith and that means a lot to Selma as it is representing Islam. "It's not a burden. I think it's a privilege really. I think representing my people or representing the masjid that I attended or representing the scarf, I think that's all a privilege. I'm grateful to have that."

CHAPTER 8

Rida's Story

> If you come to my school, you're not going to feel like it's an American school. That's not how it's designed.
>
> RIDA

• •
•

Rida's parents are originally from Pakistan. Her father came for college and her mother came here after having attended medical school in Pakistan. Her parents were married here. Rida has never visited Pakistan, because most of her family lives in America, with one set of grandparents in Virginia, and the other in Texas. Rida, the older of two sisters, was born and raised in America and went to a Muslim school from Pre-K to high school. Rida's parents chose to enroll her and her sister in a Muslim school to provide them with a religious environment that matched the values at home. Rida greatly enjoys reading everything from fiction to news articles on CNN. She enjoys learning new things independently and has taught herself new forms of exercise, including hip-hop, participates in several extra-curricular activities, like the school's debate team, soccer, Science Olympiad, Tae Kwon Do, and the Spanish Club. She feels that all learning has to have a purpose and she is always inspired to do new things. Rida is interested in pursuing medicine in the future and is waiting to hear from colleges of her choice.

1 The Role of School

A quiet young adult, Rida appears to be an introvert, but she holds strong opinions about her educational experience. Rida felt that her school could have done a better job of building a foundation of faith among students. This impacted her learning, which she felt would have been more effective had the school made a greater effort, especially with the religious studies curriculum that appeared to be haphazard to Rida and she did not think highly of the instruction.

© NOOR ALI, 2022 | DOI:10.1163/9789004519268_009

Additionally, Rida believed that the school culture was "messed up." She felt that the school lacked expertise and did not provide support in the college application and recommendation process. She felt that not only was she not prepared for the transition, but also the management did not communicate well overall. She conveyed:

> I think the management just doesn't communicate with us properly. I think they just yell at us a lot. I think they don't tell us; they don't treat us like adults. They treat us like younger children. They don't treat us like we are responsible. I feel like that's a problem because students get frustrated really easily and then there's no communication between the students and the authorities and that's a problem. They should trust us more; they should let us do things. They should allow discussion on a variety of topics like they should be so secluded. I don't know how to explain this into any difference. There's things that happen in the world and they shield us from that and we should act like we don't know about them, but that is not how it works.

Rida felt that the school's vision was to protect the Muslim identity of students by secluding them from the mainstream culture. Topics pertaining to LGBTQ, safe sex, substance abuse, or interactions between boys and girls were considered off limits for discussion. Rida felt that several students in her school were in relationships with each other, but the school opted to not discuss it because "oh it is haram" (impermissible). Rida opined that the environment was largely inflexible and refused to look at issues that were relevant to students. Instead, Rida felt that the school made a big deal about pointing out if students of the opposite gender stood or sat next to each other. Her parents were equally agitated about this mentality.

In Rida's experience the scope of the educational experience at her school was not expansive and because many instructors followed a strict code, they did not delve into conversations on many topics. In this regard, Rida opined that while it was a safe space to pray together and attend religious classes, the school "does not expand me as an American person within American culture, basically." She described the sheltered and exclusive environment as

> a very closed-off type of universe. It doesn't feel like we're very connected to the world outside. We're not like other schools. We're not as open. We're not as culturally expansive. We're not free to do similar things. We can't do the smallest things.

2   Defining Self, Race, and Popular Culture

Rida does not feel there is much Pakistani about her, except liking a few food
and clothing items, since she has never visited Pakistan. Rida identifies herself
as Muslim in that she goes to the mosque and prays. Rida feels, however that
she is American in terms of pop culture, which includes her taste in music and
shows. Rida describes herself as a "hijabi Muslim American" who is interested in
pop culture. Being a Muslim American for Rida, means having an equal opportunity for all things except one. "I think you have to work harder to show people
that you are not different from them." Rida believes that for Muslim American
women, if they wear the hijab, it is not a level playing field, because in any interaction, they start off with a strike against them through the stereotypical perceptions that the mainstream holds, which builds an immediate wall. However,
once that wall is broken, people begin to see the similarities over the differences.

Growing up, Rida believed that she was not as "cultured" into Americanness
as she is now. Her parents did not have the Disney Channel at home and the TV
was used to play videos on tape for the children. When in school, Rida would
hear other children talk about shows on the Disney Channel. Looking back,
Rida reflected that it was during her late elementary and middle school years
that she found out about American culture, which for her included movies,
TV shows, music, and food. She felt she was more American than her parents
in that she knew the cultural references better than her parents did. Over the
years her choice of food changed as well from ethnic foods like biryani (chicken
and rice) to burgers. While all this was American for Rida, she felt traditions
were what was Muslim about her. These traditions included clothing and food
choices that her family had ingrained into her, but also choices about "moral-
ity, such as how to treat other people, and concepts of humility and justice."

3   Anxiety about Transitioning to College

Rida is anxious about transitioning to college after having only been in an
Islamic school. She is hoping to find friends who would not change the way
she was. Rida shared that when she moves away from here to attend college,
she would still be doing the same things but in an environment that was now
different. She felt there were certain parts of her identity that would test her
greatly, and they all fell around areas of socialization and interaction with new
people. She shared some examples:

> I'm gonna have to go to parties; I'm gonna have to do those kinds of
> things. So how to not get sidetracked. Like, how do I know I won't drink,

or something like that later on in the future? Because I could get coerced, so I'm afraid that I won't have enough confidence to maybe keep doing the things I am doing right now.

Rida was in a deep nagging state of concern about whether she would be able to prove herself strong enough in the face of freedom, choices, and opportunities that college would have to offer, and acknowledged her self-doubt:

> There's always a chance, and I don't know myself well enough to know, 'cause I've never been in that kind of environment before; I've always been secluded in the school that I attend. It's always been the same people. It's always the same religion. So, I wouldn't know, and that's what scares me.

Despite her fears of what choices she might make, or what challenges she may face, Rida is convinced that she will not take the hijab off, because it is an absolute part of her identity. While she is afraid that someone might be harassing or discriminatory toward her due to her hijab, she has never really experienced any bigotry and feels her fear may be unfounded.

Rida was surprised at the results of the Trump presidential election, she but had faced no discrimination afterward. She believed this was because she only moved around in safe spaces, whether it be her all Muslim school, or extra-curricular activities where she had been going for several years and people knew her well. Had she been in college the experience may have been different. She shared:

> It does worry me. It worries me that I won't be able to survive on my own. It's been so secluded. I've heard stories of people who just went off on and just on a different kind because they were given so much freedom right after they left for so many rules.

Transition to college posited two challenges for Rida, one of losing faith, and the other of being outside of her comfort zone and safe space where she may be prone to discrimination.

4   Impact of Religious Values

Rida shared that she had started wearing the hijab in second grade, just like that. Her sister started wearing it when she was in fourth grade. While Rida's mother also wore the hijab, she did not tell Rida and her sister to wear it. In fact, her mother often reminded her that it was a choice she had made on her own, but that it was something to be proud of "because it made you a walking symbol of Islam." Rida felt that wearing the hijab in America was a symbol of strength, because it was done despite the rhetoric of hate. While Rida had never experienced any instances of racial hate, she had been asked the question of why she wore the scarf in safe inter-faith spaces by students of other religious associations. Her answer had been that hijab was a sign of modesty and that it protected women, and that it was not intended to oppress in any way.

Rida explained that there were things that just had to be done, regardless of whether one felt weird about it. One such example was praying in public. At the movie theater, she remembered praying in the corner with her family because it was time and they would have missed their prayer if they didn't make it right there. She felt weird doing it and thought about how she might appear to people who were not familiar with the practice; however, that did not deter her from praying in public. While several of Rida's friends would often forget about praying when the time came, but she did have one friend who reminded her when they were together. Rida also remembered times when she had prayed at the mall, by going inside one of the changing rooms. That experience was definitely more comfortable for her than praying at the movie theater.

5   The Strengthening Role of Family

Rida described both parents as practicing Muslim professionals. Her mother wore the hijab, and while she had not forced Rida and her sister to wear it, both girls decided to wear it in grades two and four respectively. Because Rida was very young when she wore it, she could not remember if it was due to the modeling of her mother. She did know, however, that her mother had stressed that wearing it meant you became a representative of the religion as a whole and that was something to be proud of. After having taken Arabic at her school until 8th grade, Rida was done with it, so she opted for Spanish in high school on her mother's suggestion. Rida holds her mother advise dear to her around several issues. When it comes to interacting with people:

> My mom would always tell me that once you meet people or people in public and if they do happen to be discriminatory, once you start talking to them and they see that you are just like them. They will start to accept you.

When the school did a mediocre job at building a faith foundation, Rida felt her parents had taught her more about daily Islamic living than the school, because they had a more balanced and practical approach to living faith. When Rida was fined for inappropriate clothing at school, she felt that her family's understanding was more flexible than that of the school. She felt the school was in "overkill" mode with instruction. "I feel like these things that I learned at home from my parents are more effective and stuck with me way more than the things I learned at school." Her family prayed in congregation at home, with their father leading them. When vacationing together, the family made time to pray together as well. At home religious supplications could be found posted everywhere as reminders. Because there are religious supplications for daily tasks like eating, stepping in or out of the house, drinking water, going to the bathroom, etc., her parents tried to remind the children of inculcating these practices into their daily lives. The family fasted together and made a concerted effort to build family bonds around religious practice. Rida referred to these as life lessons from her family that ranged all the way from identity building, faith in practice, relationships, and interactions.

Between her parents, she felt it was her mother who was more American since her father was not as adept about American culture and did not get many of its references. Highlighting their cultural differences, in their home there were two cuisine preferences. Her father wanted ethnic food and the children wanting American. Determining the spectrum of acculturation and placing oneself on it is an act performed adeptly.

CHAPTER 9

Layla's Story

> Islam isn't just a religion; it's a lifestyle. So when it comes to things like the environment, there are practical reasons that we should care and there are also religious reasons that we should care, but these two coexist, they go hand in hand.
>
> LAYLA

∴

Layla is a 19-year-old sophomore studying chemical engineering in the Northeast. Born and raised here, her parents are ethnically Turkish. Her father was born in America, whereas her mother moved to the United States from Turkey because she was not allowed to wear the hijab there in university. Layla felt that her parents supported her extremely well and encouraged her in all her academic pursuits and had taught her that anything was possible when she set her mind to it.

1   Navigating Identity

When asked to identify herself, Layla described herself as a Turkish, female, Muslim hijabi. "I don't consider myself a person of color; I do consider myself white." When asked if she used American as part of her identity, she responded "not normally," because:

> Ever since I was younger, my mom always instilled in me that, there's a reason that we don't behave like my friends who weren't Muslim. There's a reason that I don't dress the same. So, I've never truly considered myself American until maybe more recently, but still not something that I've truly grasped.

Layla recalled:

> When I was younger and I had first started to wear [the] hijab it affected me more deeply. Now it's just really a way of life. When I was younger, I

would think that people were looking at me or judging me, and now I don't feel that I'm treated differently from others, really.

She continued, "I've had some encounters where people were more judgmental to my face, but they're usually isolated incidents and I wouldn't say that it reflects most people I've encountered." Layla mentioned that she does "some things that people would consider awkward, like you know, praying and washing my feet and things like that, but for the most part, I don't think that it's harmed me really." In fact, Layla felt that her identity had some positive impact in the sense that she feels "that I am more inclined to do things without much regard for others' opinions." She went on to say, "Earlier it did impact me a bit negatively, because I was very unsure of my identity and myself, and my right to exist in a way, or my right to take up space, but I have come to terms with that." When Layla was younger, she often felt she was not considered American enough, but "now I personally find that I feel a little bit jaded because I don't follow fashion trends." She also shared that she is happiest when she is just "who I am." Additionally she related that "this idea of being 'American enough' has a very arbitrary definition. What is America? What is our understanding of what it means to be an American because I think there are many different types of 'American.'"

Layla also felt that there was judgement in the Muslim community about how Muslim someone was. She shared an incident when:

> an older Muslim student from the MSA came to talk with me about the fact that she had seen me talking to a male classmate a lot. This made me very uncomfortable because it [was] presumptuous and I didn't expect to be judged for my behavior, come under scrutiny, especially in college.

2   Educational Journeys

Layla went to a Muslim elementary and middle school, where she felt her "learning was accelerated due to small class sizes" and there was a "personal touch there" in the years of her life which she considered "transformational." She felt that she had been "well supported" in those years of her life which contributed to her academic success afterwards.

For Layla, her transition to public high school was challenging in terms of being comfortable with her identity. She "was receiving the most criticism" by:

some people at school who weren't very understanding of the fact that other people exist and other cultures exist. One person, when I was fasting in Ramadan, would constantly remark about how dangerous and unhealthy it was. When I explained the practices of how you have to wash yourself, I got comments from someone who said that it was a third world thing.

Because Layla wore the hijab, some people acted shocked that I had hair underneath. "Some people demanded to see it. There was once a classmate who saw my hair in the bathroom and described it to some of the males in my class." Layla recalled a time when she was asked if she "owned any shorts at all." Layla shared that incidents like that made her "very uncomfortable with expressing who I was, and I felt like I had to hide or be less conspicuous." In those days, Layla began to pay less attention to her health and "how I was treating myself. I was less inclined to keep myself polished – my goal was just to study and get out at the end of the day." In high school, Layla was a part of several clubs and volunteer activities and those gave her a "level of confidence and a sense of belonging." Sports in her high school years were problematic mostly due to her clothing, when for example, her lacrosse coach asked if she would wear shorts, or while swimming, an elderly gentleman told her she would swim faster if she wasn't held down by her clothing. While there were some times when she would get complimented on her hijab by strangers, she recalled a time when her brown Muslim friend was told in a public setting "we walk on the right side of the railing in America."

Layla's high school experience was situated in two places: a diverse public high school and a smaller college preparatory high school. In both places the experience of praying remained similar. "It's a little bit embarrassing, but you get over it. Sometimes there are people there, so we'd have to find someplace else to pray. I felt very exposed and uncomfortable." Muslim students, including Layla, often have to make a request with administration to be given a space to pray or when requesting any religious accommodation. About that experience, she shared:

> To be frank it's always been embarrassing to bring up that [I] need to pray. Also, I think it goes hand in hand with this idea that I found true, especially for children of immigrants, or immigrant people themselves, where they feel that they have to feel grateful, or that they don't have as much of a right to take up space, which is completely false.

Contrary to her high school experiences, Layla felt more comfortable in college. She shared,

> I feel more liberated, because I can actually choose with whom I can interact, whereas in high school you're confined to a building; you have set times to do everything. You can't really change who you have to see or interact with on a daily basis.

She felt that in college she had the choice to surround herself with positive people. Layla also tried her hand at fencing and boxing in college. Fencing

> was something that I've never had the courage to try before in high school because I was always afraid, like, what if I suck. That's embarrassing. But in college, I was just like okay well I don't care, I'm just gonna try it.

While Layla perceived that she did not have real friendships in middle and high school, but that she was connecting better with her friends in college because of "similar mindsets, work ethics" and she felt they "were supportive of each other's worldly and other worldly pursuits." Layla met some friends through the MSA and conversations about religion were a welcoming experience.

3   Classroom Conversations

Layla was able to keep her religious identity separate from her formal education, "especially because I'm in a STEM field, where when you present your work, you tend to be very faceless or it's more about the work than the person itself." In a class on the Modern Middle East, and for the first time since her Muslim school days, she came across a teacher:

> who has an actual respect and humility when talking about the vast complexity of the Middle East, which is a predominantly Muslim area of the world. I really appreciate the way that she talks about the complexity of the whole region and how she warns the general student to be very open minded and humble when it comes to addressing this part of the world, and to keep your biases back and I do appreciate, like, her passion and integrity and open mindedness.

Her college experience was such a contrast to her high school experience where they "just talk about the fall of the Ottoman Empire and WWI and the presentation of the Middle East is vastly through a Western lens." Layla also reflected that when they discussed "prominent figures in American history who have been Muslim, like Muhammad Ali or Malcolm X, they tend to brush over their Muslim identity."

Thinking about her high school classroom conversations, Layla pondered:

> Sometimes I wonder if when I feel uncomfortable in discussions, if it's
> me projecting an expectation of others to not be understanding, or if it's
> actually the case. I find that can impact my viewpoint of things, which
> is why I have tried to take my identity out of it so as to prevent that bias
> within myself and to make myself more comfortable. When it [came] to
> discussions about 9/11, I found that my peers have been very understand-
> ing and I haven't really had the experience, where, like everyone in the
> classroom looks at the one who is hijabi. If conflict does arise, it's usually
> because of people's general lack of understanding for how I dress, but it
> was often more prevalent in high school than it is in college.

Layla continued, "I found that in college the topics of conversation tend to
be more daring than in high school, but I've also found that people try their
hardest to be as respectful as possible." In a class on Africa where organized
religion was being talked about, "there was a moment where I felt a little bit on
the spot, because I do very publicly represent a religion." When conversations
about 9/11 took place, Layla posited:

> It was a travesty. But sometimes, I can't help but question the motives
> for why we talk about it as much as we do, mainly because of the subse-
> quent violence that the United States inflicted on the rest of the world,
> and sometimes I wonder if it's used as a justification for that. I don't par-
> ticularly get uncomfortable because I don't associate the horrible people
> who would do that with Islam. I'm aware that some people do think that,
> but for most educated people that's not the case. I wonder why we don't
> talk more about the aftermath of what the United States did after it.

When a shooting or a bombing takes place the first thought that crosses Layla's
mind is:

> I hope it's not a Muslim, because I understand that there is a precedent
> for what a Muslim looks like and I want us to be able to, like, live in peace
> in this country, and it does concern me that Muslim hate crimes aren't
> talked about as much in this country.

Layla recalled a time when Muslims were killed in a hate crime and "how long
it took to enter the mainstream media. Because of incidents like that I get

nervous, and I don't want there to be any more ammo for that kind of think-ing." Layla was shaken by the attacks on Capitol Hill on January 6, 2021, sharing:

> When someone is in a position of power like that, their speech does mat-ter, and when his [Trump's] primary goal is to appeal to a violent and aggressive and discriminatory voter base, that doesn't make me feel very safe. Propagating these ideals and making it seem like it's patriotic is very concerning to me. It's easy to feel afraid for your life, as a Muslim, as a female; I find that it helps me live better to not think about it too hard.

4   Relationship with Hijab

Layla started wearing the hijab when she was 12 years old. She shared:

> When I came to college, I was very aware of something that I hadn't con-sidered before – that hijab isn't a decision that I make once and it's done. Living away from my parents in a dorm in college, I had to make the deci-sion to wear it every single day. It was a very conscious decision every day to put on the hijab and that's when I really realized that growing up in a Muslim family doesn't necessarily make me a Muslim; even though I was born to that family, I have to define that for myself now.

Initially, Layla had started wearing the hijab partially because of her family, but she:

> had been considering wearing it even before. I can't exactly understand the reason that was going through my 12-year-old mind at the time, but it was just something that an adult Muslim woman does, and I did grasp that not everyone did it, but I knew that I wanted to be of the demo-graphic that does.

When asked if she finds it hard sometimes, Layla responded:

> There are times when I experience doubt or when I wonder what my life would be like without it. There have been times that I struggle, or won-dered what life is like on the other side, but I've always stuck with it. And I'm glad I have. I'm sure they'll also be times in the future, when I have that same doubt, but I hope that I'll always have the courage to keep it up.

5   Religion as Lifestyle

Being Muslim deeply impacts career choices for Layla. As she thought about chemical engineering, she has different pathways to consider:

> I promised myself that I would never get into petroleum or weaponry, even though they would be lucrative, because of my beliefs that our environment is so important; it's not something that I would want on my conscience. I've always believed that Islamic faith and science go hand in hand. I've always found religious reasons as well as practical reasons to not pursue weaponry or environmental. Islam isn't just a religion; it's a lifestyle. So, when it comes to things like the environment, there are practical reasons that we should care and there are also religious reasons that we should care, but these two coexist, they go hand in hand.

Layla also followed the lifestyle practices (sunnah) of the Prophet Muhammad, that makes "practical and religious sense, like I'm eating foods that are local and in season." This holds great relevance because oftentimes a dissonance is felt with practices of Prophet Muhammad from fourteen centuries ago to contemporary existence. Muslims will often explain the benefit of a prophetic practice through science to validate its application.

CHAPTER 10

Samreen's Story

I'm afraid of people's perception of what Islam is and who Muslims are, because I don't want to ever be afraid of being who I am.
SAMREEN

∴

Samreen is an 18-year-old college freshman studying biology in New England. Her parents are originally from India and they moved here for work. When asked to describe her identity, Samreen said, "I would consider myself to be Indian American and a practicing Muslim." She felt that in her daily life, she sees "things in a way that other people might not be able to see because of my Indian or Muslim background." Her identity also impacted her choice of people she surrounded herself with and the activities she was a part of. Samreen had diverse and robust experiences from being on the equestrian team, the Muslim Students Club, Black History Committee, Asian Culture Club, and Amnesty International. Horseback riding holds a special place in Samreen's heart. "It's not just horseback riding; it's the idea of spending time with the horse and learning more about things like equine therapy."

1   Being Impacted: School and Family

Samreen had attended a Muslim elementary and middle school and felt that her religious education there had emphasized to her the need for volunteering. She engaged in several volunteer activities as a result of that exposure. She wanted that religious education to also remain a part of her when she transitioned to the local public high school. In middle school, "things like praying were part of the schedule," but in high school, she "had to figure that out on [her] own, which was completely different" and it took a while for her "to figure out how to make it work."

Samreen felt that being Muslim gave her opportunities of being in a club, interacting with other Muslims, learning from them, and learning about other variations of Islamic practice.

© NOOR ALI, 2022 | DOI:10.1163/9789004519268_011

Samreen did not go to the mosque that often, but she did find it to be a comfortable place where she could focus on her relationship with God and meet community members.

Samreen shared that it was in high school when she realized that a lot of Muslim students "didn't care as much as I did about praying" and it was the Muslim school that she had gone to where she had learned the importance of praying. Samreen's father is Muslim and her mother is Hindu and that allowed her "to see those different opinions and decide for myself what I believe in." Samreen felt that living in this environment taught her about:

> being kind to others about their beliefs. I've learned what to say and what not to say in certain settings, to respect them when they go to the temple or do certain things that I might not understand or find funny. I know how to hold myself back. My mom has always been very open about talking about these things, but a big thing was wearing the hijab. It was something that I always thought I would do, but it was always something that my mom didn't want me to do, so it was a conflict in my mind.

Wearing the hijab was part of Samreen's uniform in middle school and it "felt special" to her. She knew that her father would be supportive, but she found it to be a "bit of a struggle" in terms of her mother. However, in high school, she decided not to wear the hijab because she didn't want it to affect her relationship with her mother and her family.

Samreen home was shared with one of her grandparents. Having a grandparent at home taught Samreen to make time daily to connect with her. She would pray and read with her when time permitted. They watched movies together and Samreen translated them for her. She also shared incidents with her grandparent to get her perspective on things.

In high school, Samreen had a Muslim friend she'd known since middle school that she was very close to. She found it to be very helpful that they had similar identities and thought in similar ways. Samreen made one new Muslim friend in high school as well and the three of them have journeyed together into college.

Samreen noticed that in high school that there were many students she knew who were Muslim, but they did not show up to the Muslim club meetings. Yet, several others who she didn't know would show up. Samreen recalled an incident that she found particularly sad. Samreen ran into a girl she knew to be Muslim and asked her (in the presence of another person) if she would come to the next MSA meeting. The Muslim girl looked pleadingly at Samreen as if to say please don't tell the other student what MSA stands for because she didn't want her religious identity disclosed. "She wanted me to lie for her, and I just didn't know what was happening." The girl covered up Samreen's question by giving the acronym, MSA, another meaning. Samreen was caught off guard because:

> I didn't know this was such a big deal, it's never been such a big deal for people to know that I'm Muslim, so that was the first time was kind of shocked to see someone trying to hide that fact … you see a lot of that in high school, people trying to hide the fact that they're Muslim.

Samreen attributed this fear to media portrayal. "People have a certain view of what being Muslim is, and no one takes the time to explain to them anything about Islam." They have these views based on the news or what their parents have said that:

> Islam is not a great religion, and then these people don't want to defend their religion, because they want to be friends with these people, so they'd rather be on their good side and I guess being on their good side means not being Muslim.

Samreen spoke about her transition to a public high school and said,

> Fasting in high school was a whole different experience. There's also a conflict with Eid being on the day of a final, which is something we had to go and talk to administration about because we want to help everyone else out who wanted to spend Eid in the mosque in the morning. We had to fight for [it] and have important conversations about these things in high school.

Other than these examples, Samreen felt her transition to high school was fairly easy, made very comfortable because she had friends. She also felt that because both her friends wore the hijab and were easily identifiable as Muslim, she found courage in keeping her identity strong.

2   Being American

Samreen opined that the mainstream perception of what it meant to be American was to be white, so she did not come across as being American enough. Even for herself "it was hard; like a concept, I had to learn that I was American, too." She felt that this self-awareness occurred around 2016, when politics were discussed. Before that she had never paid attention or cared about them, but around 2016 identity took center stage because of the bigotry of the election. Samreen now thinks she is American enough and feels it's important for people to know that she is just as American as they are.

Samreen offered that because she did not wear the hijab, some Muslims might consider her to not be Muslim enough and think "she doesn't care" or "she's not modest." Interestingly, Samreen also noticed:

> when they think that you're not Muslim enough, they think that they can tell you anything. Like they'll talk to you about their feelings about boys or something like that. I feel I was sheltered from many such things and other girls who I know who went to public school were not. When they share those things with me, I don't know what to say and it's always very awkward, because I don't know what you expect me to say. They expect you to agree with them; it's always hard to speak the truth or speak your opinion.

On the reverse end, Samreen also felt that she was judged to be too Muslim by other Muslims for being in a leadership position in the Muslim club. Regarding some Muslim kids that she had gone to middle school with, she relayed:

> I see them doing things I never thought they would do, but they do; and I think they think that based on who I hang around with, there are certain things that they have to do, or they must do. There was a situation where one of my friend's brothers was posting something weird on Instagram. He was with the girls and he didn't want me and my friends to see, so he purposely has his friends unfollow us so that we wouldn't see what they were doing because they didn't want us to know about it, because they thought we were so Muslim and we would go and complain and make a big thing out of it.

3   Uncomfortable Conversations

In the classroom Samreen discerned:

> that the teacher was very hesitant about certain topics, especially when it came to Islam, because I think she was afraid of getting it wrong. In the classroom, actually, we had a couple Muslims. I would feel like I had to

say something to correct her if something is wrong, but I also don't want to make her feel uncomfortable because she is the teacher. That's always something that I feel when it comes to the topic of religion.

She also opined:

> If we get to the topic of religion or politics, these are things that teachers don't like to talk about and I've been in situations where a teacher will take a political side, and that will upset people, and this will become a big issue.

Samreen was surprised that even though her high school had had a diverse student population, there were students who were Trump supporters. She remembered a time when a teacher said something against Trump and two white girls were upset about it. "They didn't do anything about it, but I heard them complaining about it among themselves and I just sat there and heard them, and it was odd because I had just assumed everyone had the same opinion as me." Samreen felt good when there were conversations about Gandhi because she felt that these were her people being taught in class.

When conversations about 9/11 take place:

> I always feel like people are staring at me, and I think, oh no, this is about me, although it's really not. I wasn't there (when it happened). This is an idea that always annoys me, just because a group of Muslims did something wrong, they say all Muslims are doing wrong, and I feel because you're Muslim, it's kind of your fault.

The first thought that crosses Samreen's mind when there is an act of violence is, is the perpetrator "Muslim or Christian? Because I'm afraid of people's perception of what Islam is and who Muslims are, because I don't want to ever be afraid of being who I am." She added:

> I have done nothing wrong, but all of a sudden, to be seen as someone who does something wrong just because of what I believe in or my beliefs, it just doesn't feel right to me; it doesn't sit well, and it scares me knowing that I could be judged based off of this.

Samreen recalled a time when she was younger and a neighbor that she used to play with asked her if she was Muslim and if that meant that she was bad. "I was confused. I didn't know why she would think that and it didn't make much sense to me. But as I grew older, when I remember that conversation, now I know what that means." When her hijabi friend and she were volunteering at a hospital, a patient screamed at her friend and called her "a mother fucker, and he was so loud I could hear him outside the room. When I'd walked into the room, I had no issue. But when my friend walked in, there was this issue because of her hijab."

Sometimes for Samreen, identity came in the way of doing things. In making plans with her friends, they had to give one of her friend's parents a week's notice and it was usually her friend's father's choice if he would let her go out or not. Another friend with a male sibling was given an earlier curfew than her brother was given. "That's always strange to me because it doesn't seem fair to me."

Samreen concluded that being an Indian American Muslim:

> Gives me an advantage. I'm understanding and more sympathetic towards others because, I get to see things that other people might not get to see or experience, and I think being sympathetic towards others is very important because sometimes people tend to be harsh to others, and because we don't understand what they're going through.

Yasmine's Story

I wanted people to know, yes, I am Muslim. We're not crazy; we're normal people.

YASMINE

∴

Yasmine is a college junior from the Northeast studying communication, business, and education. She was born and raised in the United States, but her parents were originally from South Asia. Yasmine is a foodie, loves socializing, bubble tea, and desserts. Yasmine always identifies herself in four ways saying, "I'm a Pakistani American Muslim woman. I want people to know that I'm South Asian and a Muslim woman before saying that I'm American."

1   Acculturation

When Yasmine travels to her parent's country of origin, the language barrier and the accent with which she speaks the language makes her appear whitewashed and "so American" to the relatives. Yet in America, she is considered a person of color and "so brown" and feels she "doesn't fit in." She explained that there is a "split identity and this conflict is something that everybody goes through when they grow up [in America] and have a different background." She explained the conflict further by sharing:

> Honestly, it's also because I'm not whitewashed. For example, I have an earliest memory from elementary school, like, this is the earliest memory of really feeling it. I had a group of friends and they were all white girls, except for one girl. She was Asian ... her family was from China, but she herself never spoke Chinese, like, she wasn't very attached to her roots. I remember every summer all those girls would go to the Cape and they would go together with their families and they would all say, 'Oh, you should come,' but I would never get an actual invite. I remember even

© NOOR ALI, 2022 | DOI:10.1163/9789004519268_012

feeling back then there's something fishy going on here and I don't think it's necessarily because I'm a person of color, but because I'm a person of color that is close to my roots and heritage … being Muslim has never been anything I've wanted to hide.

Despite the conflict of identity, she wants to remain close to her heritage and the ethnic language and to pass it on to her children, but she felt that she was losing on that front. It is often hard for Muslim Americans who have another language to be able to maintain proficiency in it when mainstream existence is devoid of it.

2   Values

In her daily life, Yasmine tries to be "a good person and making sure I'm doing the right thing and trying to be God-conscious." Diversity at the college campus made it easier to feel comfortable in her skin, but the college experience also allowed her to get a little sidetracked from her faith. She felt the COVID19 lockdown allowed her to recenter her life.

> Growing up in a white and wealthy town, I had a hard time. Around 9/11 everyone would look at you. I know of a Muslim family that had pork thrown outside their house and I was very shocked at that. In my own experience I've mostly had subtle comments or looks. In high school I had a teacher, he was Jewish and gay, and he would always bring up Palestine and Israel. The teachers in my school were mostly white, but I had one teacher who was Indian-Muslim and she wore the hijab. She's like my favorite person and I'm so thankful, because she really pushed me to realize and make meaning of all the subtle things that happened and [helped me] understand that it's not going to go away and learn what you can do about it. She was great; she was young and had grown up in California. She had experiences like mine so she helped me in so many ways. Anytime something was going on at home, I would talk to her about it because she would understand that – the immigrant experience, our parents' mentality.

Yasmine realized that this was the exception and that she got lucky to be in a white and wealthy town that had a teacher who was brown and hijabi. Her relationship with this mentor was life-altering in many ways. She could vent to her, seek help about college applications, talk about her lived experiences, and be understood. This mentor helped start up a Muslim affinity group and helped the students navigate their lived experiences after the Trump election:

> I can't even explain how she helped me socially. She was savage; she was not afraid to call people out. She really allowed for me to just feel more comfortable with myself and in my skin and just be open about the identities I care about.

Yasmine recalled a time in middle school when she was sitting in class when a male student said, "All Muslims are terrorists." This was Yasmine's first encounter with outright bigotry:

> Lucky for me, the other kid who was sitting there said to him, 'Dude, don't say that; that's messed up.' Just having somebody say that is a huge thing, because otherwise I would have just been quiet or shocked. But I basically got a pass on my first time because somebody was brave enough in sixth grade to say something.

Though Yasmine remains involved in the MSA, but she shared that it was in actuality the Mosque and Sunday School that played the greatest role in shaping her identity. Yasmine went to a public school throughout, so her religious identity was shaped by the mosque. She reminisced how when they were younger, they used to dread going; but when they grew older and it was time to graduate from Sunday School, she was sad because she just wanted to stay as part of the community. The transition to really liking Sunday School happened in 9th grade, when they put together a youth group. The children had always been separated by gender and it was with the youth group that they could finally just "talk to each other, and it was normal and we would have a good time – even though there'd be helicopter adults. We all went to different high schools, but we all had the same experience of being that minority and like what we did about it." The mosque remains a safe community space for Yasmine.

Yasmine also felt that her mother has made her the person that she is. Her mother would remind her to pray always. She felt because she was an older child, her parents were more vigilant with her, speaking to her in the native language, putting her in Sunday School to learn to read the Arabic of the Quran, etc., while her younger sibling was not given all these opportunities. Yasmine felt that her father was not very religious and she wanted to be more religious but struggled with it. Staying at home during the pandemic made it hard for her to stay connected to faith which she did through the MSA. "My family definitely has a hands-off" approach and Yasmine learned many basic things about her faith in terms of rituals through her MSA group. Yasmine added,

> When I was younger, my dad would tell me not to tell people that I'm Pakistani because it is associated with a Muslim majority. There was a video that was going viral of this little girl who wore a hijab and she was treated really bad by the kids at school, and when my dad saw it, he said I can't tell anybody I'm Muslim. I understand it was out of concern for safety and wanting to protect your kid, but that pushed me to, like, tell people even more because I wanted people to know, yes, I am Muslim. We're not crazy; we're normal people.

Yasmine felt that in her freshman year of college, she had lost some interest in her faith and wasn't connected spiritually to the ritual practices:

> Honestly, I don't know why and I'm upset that it happened – also everything happens for a reason. Like now, I feel like I've bounced back even stronger in my faith and I'm really happy about that, and I think my friends had a huge impact because, these MSA kids, they come from families where Islam is a huge thing in their household and that's been refreshing to see again.

Yasmine shared that friends make all the difference. When it was people around her who emphasized their South Asian identity, so did she; and now when she is involved with the MSA folks, her Muslim identity is finding strength.

Diversity does play a key part in how non-white students find comfortable spaces for themselves. Yasmine recalled a time when her school was bussing other districts' public school students with concentrated Black and Hispanic populations. When she started hanging out with the new students she "felt so much more welcome and I felt I didn't need to make an effort to fit in like I did with my white friends."

3   Curriculum

For Yasmine, the curriculum taught in the educational system had inherent biases and only showed one perspective. She spoke about Martin Luther King and how, while being taught his accomplishments, the curriculum did not share "he was on the FBI hitlist; he was somebody the country did not like at all and we're glorifying him now, but acting like you were glorifying him before." As her educational experience evolved Yasmine said she was learning more about her identity and that of people of color. She felt that she had grown up "privileged" and "sheltered" and that her "socio-economic status," regardless of her lived experience as a Muslim, had given her privileges that were not the reality of her black friends:

> Academic experience has been impactful because now I'm able to put all those things into context. I'm learning about Black Lives Matter. There are so many things we don't learn about in school, that had so much to do with the government and the people who are in power at that time and it's like we just are constantly glorifying things and not taking the blame for things that we should have taken the blame for.

Yasmine shared that she had "never ever" felt herself represented in the curriculum except in one unit on Islam. She has people who follow her social media feed and she is happy that they looked to see what her political and social opinions are. She feels that she had become better at articulating herself and now she has "actual opinions on social justice issues" and can engage in "mature conversations." Yasmine knows that even though she does not wear the hijab, she clearly identified as Muslim and comes across "as a person of faith, and someone who cares a lot about Islam."

4   Experience of Demonization

Yasmine recalled the time of the Boston Marathon bombing. She had been at her friend's place and got a call from her parents to come back home right away. The media emphasized that the bomber was a Muslim and a terrorist. She knew of a young person who was from Chechnya and after the Boston bombing happened, "police officers were following and watching him in school. He was a sixth grade kid. I still get upset about it because I'm imagining if that happened to me, how would I feel." The media went to the local mosque that the bomber had gone to and Yasmine "started getting notes at the masjid and threats, so much that the mosque had to get police security." Yasmine also felt "uncomfortable" about conversations about 9/11:

> I don't want to say this in a bad way, we should acknowledge what happened because it was really awful, but it's like we taped a moment in

history and have given it such big significance. Why aren't we also focusing on the school shootings that are happening every day? 9/11 had a huge significance in terms of associating Islam to terrorism and that's never gone away and I really don't think it's going to.

CHAPTER 12

Ayesha's Story

> I feel more afraid because people would probably try to discrim-
> inate against me especially because I outwardly portray Islam by
> wearing hijab. I feel like I could become even more of a target than
> others.
>
> AYESHA

∴

Ayesha is a 20-year-old studying management and Korean in the Northeast.
She's also an ardent fan of K-Pop and Korean dramas. Born and raised in the
United States, Ayesha's family was originally from Pakistan. When asked to
describe her identity, Ayesha said, "I am a Muslim, who is Pakistani American."
Ayesha is mindful of her practice of faith:

> I schedule my day around prayers … I try to do everything the way a
> Muslim should, like when I talk to people, because I am a hijabi, I know
> I'm representing my religion everywhere I go, so it's important that I act
> in a way that would represent Islam properly and not [be] misunder-
> stood. I try my best not to curse, I refrain from doing actions that would
> make people think it's not a good religion.

1   Influence of School

Ayesha had gone to a Muslim school until college and recalls her decision to
start wearing the hijab:

> It was really hard. I was contemplating wearing a hijab since middle
> school because in school, we were always talking about topics related to
> the day of judgment and hijab is such an important part of your life, it
> kind of scares you. I had many friends who started wearing it; my mom
> started as well and so did many family members. My own conscience told
> me I should be wearing it. One day I was coming out of school (when we

left school, we would immediately rip the hijab off our head because it was a mandatory part of the girls' uniform), I took it off, and then in the car next to me there was, I mean, there was this thing that looked at me in a very weird way. I wouldn't say it was a human, but whatever it was, I just felt very unsafe and uncomfortable and something in my mind was like, I need to start wearing the hijab and later that night we went to my aunt's house and I wore the hijab since then.

Ayesha had robust extracurricular experiences from soccer, Mock Trial, community service to the Muslim Student Association where she enjoyed listening to spiritual talks, praying in congregation, and leading career readiness initiatives for Muslim students. Ayesha's school soccer team was comprised of all Muslim girls and a Muslim coach so she "never felt out of place," but "the way we dressed was different – we were the only team that wore full sleeve jerseys. We weren't even allowed to wear leggings of any sort. Yoga pants and sweatpants were okay." When Ayesha's team played against other teams, they were always the only team dressed like this but "we wanted to perform better to show others that Muslim girls can be just like other girls."

2   Values Shaped in the Home

Her parents played a significant role in shaping her identity, because they provided her with Islamic school education and they "instilled a lot of values in her." Additionally, having a younger sibling made her "be a good role model." Ayesha felt her closest friends had a deep impact on her identity as they "try the most to go out of our way to learn Islamic knowledge ... stay on the path and better ourselves as Muslims." She also had Muslim friends that veered towards non-religious activities, but her closest friends had kept her "on the path."

Ayesha felt that being in a Muslim elementary, middle, and high school gave her several opportunities to learn about her faith and partake in rituals and Islamic activities seamlessly. Her home values did not clash with those of school. Ayesha shared that normally, "when high school students to transition to college [it is different], but it was way more different going from a small school to a huge school and then going from a very Islamic setting to something that's definitely not that."

Ayesha was accustomed to using Arabic (religious) phrases and prayers in her daily conversation. However at college "I try not to use, like, Islamic words. I wouldn't say salaam to my professors, but sometimes when I'm talking to classmates and I use Inshallah a lot, I have to catch myself; I'm like wait, they wouldn't understand that." In the classroom:

> I also have to be mindful of certain things teachers say. I'm taking business ethics right now and sometimes there's a bit of clash, especially when I'm reading the readings with religion [in mind] I just have to remind myself that this these are not my beliefs, and these are just some philosophers and thinkers of the past; I feel like [I] constantly remind myself of what my faith is and who I am.

To further explain this Ayesha spoke about how she reminded herself of her religious views when studying Locke and Hobbes, or other things like "ethics and morals like don't come from religion, and personally that's not my belief, so I have to just kind of remind myself of that."

3   College Experience

Transitioning from a Muslim school environment to college was made easier for Ayesha because the campus was very diverse and because she had friends from her previous school with her. "We were all going through the same thing, so it was helpful because we all had each other." Ayesha felt that in college "it's very easy to stray away from Islam. It's easy to become a part of different social groups." So "in order to stay true to myself, I feel it's important to keep good company around me and be a part of Islamic clubs to just stay true to my identity." Ayesha opined, "If I wasn't Muslim, I would probably be in a business frat." Ayesha shared that campus diversity made the task easier:

> I have cousins who go to predominantly white schools and schools with not much diversity and they don't even have that many Muslim friends anymore and it's hard for them to stay true to their identity. A lot of them change a lot, but, for me, I feel like I haven't changed that much because of all the Muslims I'm surrounded with.

In the college classroom and:

> being a Muslim, I try to always say the right thing ... especially in classes like ethics. Professors and other students are constantly challenging your points of views and they're also trying to, in some ways, trip students up

about what is morally right and what is morally wrong. But, I feel like I already know what my morals are and what my ethics are because of my Muslim background. In terms of constantly challenging our point of views, I try to keep to my beliefs, while also remaining neutral and I don't try to really bring attention to my opinions saying that they're Islamic beliefs, just because I'm afraid that they would either shut me out or just not really listen to me. Even though they can tell that I'm Muslim, when I talk in in class using my Islamic beliefs, I don't mention where they are coming from.

4   Defending the Faith

Ayesha remembered a time when a truck drove by her hijab-wearing soccer teammates and the driver rolled down his window to yell "terrorists" to the kids. While Ayesha felt safe on her college campus, she said she felt unsafe in states that were "more red, especially places that I'm not familiar with. I sometimes do feel unsafe when I see confederate flags or Trump signs from, well, back when Trump was President." Ayesha recalled her disbelief after that election. "I was very upset. I thought 'how could this happen?' and 'how could so many people vote for him?' but there are more people who are probably [more] racist than we thought." Conversations about 9/11 in public made Ayesha feel:

> Definitely uncomfortable. When those discussions take place in classrooms or outside of classrooms, I tend to just stay quiet and listen to what people are saying. I don't know how to talk about it with non-Muslims. If I ever have to say anything related to 9/11 or terrorist attacks, I always try to make sure to point out that those are extremists and we do not associate with those types of terrorists and that's not Islam.

Ayesha felt this was an unfair burden to carry. "I feel like people should already know how to separate that, but having to explain it and tell people that constantly is tiring." When there is any shooting or bombing that takes place:

> I hope it's not someone with a remotely Muslim sounding name. That's my first thought because if it is, the 'Muslims are terrorists' narrative comes back. Sometimes it dies down and people stop talking about it and stop thinking about it, but as soon as something like that happens, and if it's someone with a Muslim sounding name, then it can become a problem and I feel like I would have to explain that all over again to

people. You don't want people misrepresenting Islam and I hate it when that happens, especially in the media.

After an event like that takes place "I feel more afraid because people would probably try to discriminate against me especially because I outwardly portray Islam by wearing hijab. I feel like I could become even more of a target than others."

Ayesha felt that she was perceived as not being American enough and was asked about how she dressed. She also noticed that people who had experienced diversity around them knew more about Islam than others who had not had that exposure. Ayesha felt different and like she didn't belong when her co-workers would make plans that involved drinking. Ayesha had never experienced blatant discrimination but remembered a time when she went to a make-up counter with her non-hijabi cousin. She was not helped at the counter by the lady who worked there, even though she was very friendly towards her cousin. Ayesha recalled times when other Muslims she knew faced discrimination, like people being surprised that they could speak English and also being called names.

Ayesha herself did not feel that she was American enough, either:

> I feel like this might be a generational thing. A lot of Americans tend to have a lot of pride and a lot of nationalism, but I'm not like that. But I also think, it has to do with my generation: Gen Z – the way we talk about America is very different than what older people say about America. I feel like we see the good and definitely the bad in American society, in government, and politics. I feel like we're not afraid to criticize America for what it does wrong.

In the Muslim community, Ayesha felt that there was also judgment on not being Muslim enough, "People definitely judge others – like 'you're too white-washed, or you're too Americanized,' but not understanding that that's how we grew up and that's what we've grown to know."

CHAPTER 13

Fatima's Story

> ... a Pakistani Muslim girl who grew up in America. These make me
> unique, so that's why I put them first and then that I grew up in
> America.
>
> FATIMA

⁝

Fatima is an 18-year-old studying biology in the Northeast. Her parents, originally from Pakistan, immigrated to Canada and then moved to the United States. Fatima shared that her father had moved from Pakistan in search of opportunities here. She prided herself for having a lot of Pakistani culture and could speak Urdu fluently because she communicated with her grandparents in the language.

1   Culture & Identity

Fatima described her identity as "a Pakistani Muslim girl who grew up in America." She felt the first two parts of that identity were very connected with each other. Fatima found she was closer to her Pakistani culture than other kids her age were, and that for most kids her age, culture and religion did not play the emphatic part that they did in her life. "These make me unique, so that's why I put them first and then that I grew up in America."

Fatima found herself to be more American than her mother. "She would expect girls to think like this, and I think like that. Simple things like going out to eat with friends, she's always like, 'Invite them over, why do you always need to go out to be with friends.'" Fatima's family frequented the mosque and she felt that this played an important part in helping to shape her identity. She started wearing the hijab in 6th grade. Living with grandparents gave her a solid foundation in the culture and language of Pakistan, as they would:

> Talk to me about their past and how they lived in the village, so I feel like
> it helped me understand where they came from or why they were the way

© NOOR ALI, 2022 | DOI:10.1163/9789004519268_014

they were. Like, my grandmother wouldn't want to waste even tissue and it's because they came from that life.

When she travels to Pakistan, she adjusts comfortably to the culture even though the amenities she is used to here are lacking there. She does feel the American part of her identity stands out more when she is there.

2   Identity & Educational Experience

Fatima went to a Muslim elementary and middle school, and even though it had children from different immigrant families, she "didn't really feel different growing up." But, it was in high school that:

> I realized there is a different world out there. I started feeling a little bit uncomfortable, like should I maybe hide this part of myself or dress a little differently. Even the hijab, it had always been a part of me but I started to notice it was there when I was in high school.

Fatima felt that language impacted the way she navigated her space. She shared:

> I learned to speak Urdu first, so when I went to school, of course I didn't know English, but I feel like even still today, I stutter sometimes while speaking English or my English just sounds a little different or I understand some things a little slower. I felt this throughout my schooling, even high school – things that other kids can understand really fast I'll just be stuck on the topic and, maybe have extra help with the teacher just to understand.

When Fatima transitioned from her Muslim middle school to the public high school, she found it to have more freedom. "You're finally enjoying the school experience that you see in like movies, but you get asked different types of questions." She remembered a time when in her freshman year, a student asked her if, when she went home, she threw the scarf off because she must be so excited to take it off. Another time when she had given a speech on the racial profiling and targeting that exists around Muslims, she was put on the spot by another student who argued with her about gun control. Fatima felt uncomfortable about it. In genera, Fatima said she felt "different," "awkward," and "uncomfortable" at different times because of her hijab. She also recalled a time when:

We were just talking and a male teacher put his arm around me. Some people were looking at me because they knew Muslims don't do that, and I just had an uncomfortable face. I tried to brush it off and ignore it, because I didn't know what to say to the teacher.

Fatima found herself somewhat represented in the curriculum when she read a text about an Asian girl whose mother followed her culture and the book talked about the differences between American and Asian culture. She found sports to be difficult to participate in, because her clothing choice was not the norm, and it largely seemed to be space where all the popular white kids were.

In high school Fatima found friends that she could relate to through the Muslim club. She related:

It was harder for me to open up in high school because my whole life, I'd been around people who I was comfortable with and then, when I went into high school, there were so many different people and I didn't know how to react sometimes, so I just stay quiet because I don't know what to say.

Fatima joined the Asian and Black History club because "all those people understood what it means to be different." She reminisced:

It's kind of funny, in my freshman year, I only had two people from my Islamic school that went into the high school and I only had lunch with one of them. She was very open and confident, so she would make friends easily and I would just be sitting around with her friends. And then, she told me one day that I can talk more so I can make friends.

Fatima was finally able to find another hijabi at high school and they clicked because, "talking to other people wasn't that same comfort level." Friends helped keep Fatima grounded to faith, sharing:

I feel it's really easy to lose your religion in a place that's not following the same religion you are, and I feel a lot of times nowadays, parents are the only ones implementing their religion and a lot of children don't want to do that because of their friends ... they want to be like their peers. Because most of my friends are religious in some way, we all understand what religion is and we're all comfortable with us being from different religions so it doesn't make me leave Islam or feel hesitant to pray.

Sharing ethnic culture and traditions with friends also made it easier to have someone to connect with. Fatima kept her friend circle very small in high school and that was one way of safeguarding her comfort zone with people who dressed like her and belonged to a similar culture.

Fatima felt being Muslim did allow her to stand out more in class and teachers would notice her. "Even if I talked to them once, they would remember my name which made me feel important and I think that's because of the hijab. They would notice me around school." She felt that in spaces where diversity was important, she was given preference.

3   Diminishing Experiences

Conversations about 9/11 always made her uncomfortable. Fatima expressed that the topic itself was uncomfortable to her and maybe it was just her assumption that people would be staring at her when conversation about it took place. Fatima felt this way because the religious identity of the terrorist attack was primarily highlighted in any coverage or documentary about it and that made her connected to it. Similarly, when any other terrorist activity happened, Fatima was most worried that it had been perpetrated by a Muslim and then the media would make it all about religious affiliation. The Trump presidential victory came as a shock to Fatima because it signified how many people supported bigotry. Fatima feared for herself because of her identifiability as Muslim. She also felt she was not considered American enough because of her choice of clothing and because it was something that a lot of young Muslim Americans did not wear. Other things that made her uncomfortable included her traditional food and choice of watching Pakistani shows that were not American choices. Fatima shared that she "wouldn't feel comfortable eating her lunch around white people." Seeking a place to pray during lunch time meant going to the administration offices and getting a key, whereas in high school you only went to that office if you were in trouble. This caused Fatima some discomfort. Fatima also recalled a time when a teacher got upset with her and wanted to give her a quiz the same day after she had returned to school from a religious pilgrimage. She also noticed that the school conducted a moment of silence when there was a shooting that took place but did not do the same when the ones killed were Muslims. When they brought this to the administration's notice, they apologized.

Fatima felt that there were some Muslim students in high school who had sidetracked from faith, and their behaviors did not match hers. "You would get questions like why can that Muslim go to prom, or why does that girl not wear hijab, or if some Muslim person was in a relationship." Fatima would feel conflicted in such situations. "You know that they're wrong in their religion, but if a person doesn't want to it's their own choice, no one's going to force them." She found it strange that Muslim students in the school, who were not as practicing as Fatima, would ignore her or avoid her in school, but they would interact normally in private or if they come across each other in the mosque.

CHAPTER 14

Sana's Story

> I feel like people don't understand that having religion as part of
> your life and then also just being a student can coexist. Sometimes,
> I feel people think it's one or the other.
> SANA

∵

Sana is a college sophomore in the Northeast. Her family is originally from
Pakistan and she prides herself in carrying that part of cultural identity. Sana
feels strongly about correct representation of Islam and opines that people
often conflate culture with religion.

1   Critical Conversations & Representing Islam

"I was called an alien in my junior year of high school" and:

> It was by someone who I was having a conversation with in my history
> class. They said, 'Aren't you an alien?' I am almost positive they were
> misinformed about what the word meant, but I was taken aback by it,
> because I had never viewed myself as any different than the peers around
> me and that made me a little bit self-aware that sometimes people in the
> classroom do look at me differently. The majority of the people in my
> class perceive me as someone who was Pakistani, just living in America.

Sana sensed that the mainstream did not consider her American enough:

> You can tell by the tone of voice and how they talk to you that they're
> perceiving you as someone who just came into the country or someone
> who's kind of inferior. It also seems that some of my friends who immi-
> grated at an older age, so they still carried the accent, were viewed as less
> educated.

© NOOR ALI, 2022 | DOI:10.1163/9789004519268_015

Additionally, she remarked that there were stigmas attached to identity:

> As an American you have to have a completely normal accent and look a certain way. There were times when I was scared to dress in my cultural clothing or even post about it on social media because it appears as FOB-by, which is called 'fresh off the boat.'

In middle and high school, she was shy about her cultural clothing, but that was not the case now. She now posts pictures of herself in cultural clothing on social media and realizes that people are "really interested in that and I'm really proud to put that out there. Like, this is a unique form of the way we dress and I'm really proud of it and I'm glad to be able bring a lot of my everyday life here."

While Sana had mostly positive experiences, she remembered that in her freshman year at high school, "I was called Osama bin Laden's daughter by one person who I thought to be my friend and, at the time, I didn't really see that much harm in it." Sana thought of it like a joke then, but as she "grew up, I realized how harmful that statement was. And the fact that someone was even thinking something like that shows how sometimes they do correlate the fact that I'm Pakistani with those types of ideals, like extremism." On days when 9/11 was talked about "I would get stares in the classroom. I don't know if they were doing it on purpose, but it was definitely something I experienced year after year." Sana knows that a handful of extremists do not represent all practicing Muslims, but this is often conflated by others outside her faith. For the large part, Sana felt people in her state currently were not as prejudiced, but "I know my parents definitely feel differently about it. They have had more backlash with it than I do, especially in the workplace."

Sana recalled another time during high school about 9/11 when a teacher asked her in class "to explain a little bit." Later, the teacher told Sana that her intention was more "to clear up the fact that there was not a linkage between Islam and 9/11. In the moment when she had said it, I was really confused as to why she was asking me to explain in the first place." Sana felt the teacher's perception of Islam changed over the four years that Sana was there. Earlier on she had asked Sana, "Are all women forced by their fathers into wearing the hijab?" Sana then explained to her the difference between culture and Islam:

> She also had misconceptions about feminism in Islam and how women were portrayed, and that was something that I personally had to do more research about because I wanted to make sure I represented it accurately.

After I had all the facts, I was able to go and tell her that this is actually what feminism in Islam means: that women are so highly regarded in Islam; [given] all the property rights; how Islam was the first religion to give these financial property rights to women, that Islam was actually the first religion that had laid all of that out, and very, very detailed in terms of divorce. Then she was very apologetic and said, 'Thank you so much for educating me; I actually had no idea.' She thought that we weren't allowed to drive cars and everything and I explained to her the difference between culture and Islam, which is what I've had to explain to many people. I feel they have common misconceptions with that and, honestly, I don't really blame them because, if I were to view Islam the way that society and social media portrays it, I would have the same view. I think it just takes people who are willing to actually explain the way that religion is practiced and what it actually represents. It's meant to be a peaceful religion, where killing one man is like killing all of mankind. So how can these people who kill thousands of people on a daily basis represent Islam? That's the line between extremists and us. So, I feel all it takes is a little bit of education; I've seen that's made all the difference between me and the people that I surrounded myself with who are non-Muslim.

Overall, Sana felt that she was not represented in the curriculum and wished that there had been more inclusive education about Ramadan and Eid so people would know more about their Muslim classmates. "Everybody knows about Christmas, but I've rarely ever heard about this month-long event that a good number of high school students are involved in." These experiences in high school now shape the way she presents herself in college. She shared:

These are all people who I've never met before and they have absolutely no background of where I am from. I get to choose how I represent myself from scratch to everybody around me here, which is obviously something that I love, because I felt like I had the chance to completely recreate the person that I represented myself as. I knew that the only way I want to represent my identity and my religion was in a positive light, and in a way that I didn't bash people for having miseducation about it, but simply to inform. So, if somebody, who down the line, were to say, 'Oh, I knew someone who was Muslim,' I hope that the view that they have is positive because I feel all it takes is one person for you to change your mindset. I understand that when I'm talking about Islam, I'm not representing myself, I'm representing the religion as a whole.

Sana shared that in high school and in college, a lot of non-Muslims had several misconceptions about Muslim women in particular. She had been asked:

> 'Why don't you wear the hijab?' or they would say about a hijabi friend, 'I would love to see her without her hijab,' or they would say 'are you allowed this back home?' I feel like they automatically have this perception that my dad was super over the top, controlling me in everything and I kind of had to explain to them that culture is very different from what religion is.

Sana shared that a hijabi friend was asked by an older man in a store to take off her scarf. When you wear the hijab it's "the first thing people notice when they look at you and you represent Islam, which is honestly very beautiful." But then, it also "calls for these types of people to (based on what I've heard) as an invitation, to take lashes at you."

2   Extra-curriculars and Identity

Sana was a part of the student government and felt it was important for first generation Pakistani Muslims on campus to be represented because "if there is a time where our voice needed to be louder, then we would have someone there to make sure that's represented." Another organization that Sana was active in served mental health issues and Sana joined it because she wanted to advocate for this especially because in her "culture, mental health has a stigma and oftentimes people are told to pray it off, when there's an actual mental disorder that needs to be treated." Sana remained engaged in the Muslim and Pakistani associations because "it's just super important to make sure I stay connected with people" and also she likes trying new activities like rock climbing "to maintain activity and balance in my daily life, so it's not all school."

Sana did not feel that her identity obstructed her from any opportunities or sports. In fact she felt that she was given additional opportunities since she stood for an underrepresented group in science. It became difficult to enter groups in college that were "predominantly white in terms of their leadership and you can feel small having your voice heard." Also "drinking, smoking, and sex makes it hard when you know you're Muslim and can't be involved in this type of stuff." For the most part, Sana felt peers at her college were respectful and she personally did not have any problems. However, she went on to say:

> But there have been definite times that you feel you're being excluded because your views are different than others. You can be seen often as

very extremist for your views. Even if you say you are praying five times a day now suddenly people think you're super religious, which is a big thing that I've seen around here. I feel like people don't understand that having religion as part of your life and then also just being a student can coexist. Sometimes, I feel people think it's one or the other.

Thinking back, Sana recalled her time in high school where she was sometimes not considered religious enough by her peers in the Muslim students' club:

I felt pushed or turned away because I wasn't practicing the way that everybody else was practicing and I feel in high school everybody is at very different points in terms of Islam. Because there's such an identity crisis at that age, there are times where faith is the last thing on your mind and I understand that. I just wish, even if we were all at different points in our faith, that at least our one goal is to come closer to it. So, I'm hoping that the younger generations and club takes it upon themselves to make sure they foster that community, because at the end of the day, they are representing the Islamic and Muslim community and most non-Muslims there genuinely had a negative outlook what the Muslim community is. I feel like as Muslims, it's our job to make sure that we are presenting the community the way that we should be representing Islam, but it comes across as judgey and exclusive and I feel that is not the right approach.

3   Being Enough

When Sana traveled to Pakistan, she felt that she was too American for them. About those trips she shared:

I felt like I didn't belong there, but then, at the same time, I felt like I also didn't fully belong in America, that typical identity crisis. But after visiting there for many, many years, when I now go, it feels like I can fully express that part of myself without having to feel constricted. I can speak Urdu fluently, but I want to learn how to read it. I want to learn the slang, but over there, they're asking me how to be more American and now everybody else around me is wearing jeans, but all I want to do is wear my cultural clothes, so it's a weird paradox effect at this point now. Now, more than before I feel comfortable when I go there, but there's definitely a time where I had a very weird accent when I would speak or go back to Pakistan. The people could see that and they were treating me differently.

Sana felt that the local Muslim community "100% judge" for not being Muslim enough. "Surprisingly grownups, more than people my age, [say] that I'm not practicing my religion or I'm not doing enough, that I'm doing way too little, and then I've become an Americanized version of a Muslim." Sana shared that the adults "have grown up in a predominantly Muslim country and then they shifted here versus me. I've grown up in a place where I have always been a minority as a Muslim" and that:

> They looked down upon me for the clothes that I wear. It's really weird to think that as Muslims, we are supposed to keep that judgment to ourselves, and if we do want to advise someone, we do it privately. I respect the guidance, but there are people you just straight out judge.

Sana recalled:

> Receiving backhanded compliments 'your jeans are too tight' or when she went to the mosque 'oh, you decided to come and pray today,' or 'you went to the prom at your school,' as if any of those things makes me less of a Muslim than they are. I understand that there are lines and things that I still have to learn about how to be better be a better Muslim, but I also don't personally feel like it's their place as someone I don't know at all to judge me for that and put me in my place. The relationship as a Muslim is between me and Allah and that's never going to change. That is very personal to me. Whatever mistakes, I made that's between me and Him. I feel in our community it happens a lot that people still think that [because] I grew up in America, I am not practicing my faith correctly or I'm not as Muslim, as they are.

Sana found the mosque to have been a place of comfort, learning, and the community coming together. She reminisced about many good conversations at the mosque and greatly enjoyed praying through the night there during the month of Ramadan. For example:

> I love the fact that everybody can stand for hours and hours and just listen to the Quran. It brings the most overwhelming piece of comfort that I've ever felt and that never changes, like every single year. Like, life will hit you in one way or another, but [it's] that one consistency in my life when I know that I can always just go back to that place of peace.

Sana spoke highly of her father. She shared:

> I feel like a lot of girls have had bad experiences with their dad pushing
> them in the wrong manner, but my dad has always only treated me the
> way he treats my brother or that he knows that we are equal. So, I feel
> like that has given me a really strong foundation for making sure that
> Islam is represented in that way. My parents have taught me how to pray.
> They've fostered an Islamic environment in the household and they've
> never forced anything upon me. I forced [myself] to learn on my own and
> become closer to Allah, because one thing I know, that is no matter how
> much someone pushes you to pray unless you are praying for you and
> yourself, it's a different story.

Sana shared, "I have had my fair share of experiences with friends who have
tried to take me off the right track or they've tried to downplay when I would
say that I wanted to go pray." Sana had been in friends' circles where her peers
did not find the commitment to religious practice particularly serious. In her
senior year of high school and in college she began to surround herself with
friends who had similar religious orientations to her, because she wanted to
grow her faith and practice. Sana shared that her roommate was non-Muslim
but very respectful of her religious practices.

CHAPTER 15

Farah's Story

> I will always be true to my Muslim identity and my morals, but I think I present myself as very much American versus Muslim American.
>
> FARAH

∴

Born and raised in the United States, Farah is a 19-year-old studying biology in the Northeast. Her parents were originally from Indian Kashmir. She describes herself as "multi-faceted," loves to learn about anything and everything, holds "a pretty positive outlook on life," and has an "exceedingly optimistic view." Farah recalls having moved a lot and therefore making new friends quite often. She shared how supportive her family had always been and encouraged and supported in trying out different things.

1   Impact of Culture and Faith

Farah also thought about her race, religion, and culture as "big parts of my identity, at least internally, if not externally." Farah explained:

> Religion, for me, is obviously very personal. It's not something that I very much like to share with friends at college and things like that. So, I guess it's more part of my internal identity, but, of course, I am pretty open about my culture with everyone. If I had to define myself, I think it's very American. I very much think of myself as more American than Kashmiri because, if anything, I've only gone on vacation to Kashmir. I have a lot of connections to that culture, because my parents are really good at incorporating that and reminding us of that often. I very often feel much more American than Kashmiri.

© NOOR ALI, 2022 | DOI:10.1163/9789004519268_016

Also, Farah felt that being judgmental was a part of her culture. "I'm pretty much the least judgmental person you'll meet, but it's definitely something I had to unlearn."

When asked if her religious and ethnic identity impacted her daily life, Farah felt that it was more at a subconscious level. "For example, I'm Muslim, and a lot of my friends here are not. So, a lot of times I will think of things through a Muslim lens, not that I would ever mention it, but I think 'I would never do that.'" Farah felt that having a religious lens significantly played into how she made choices. For example:

> No drinking – but it's not hard for me because that's something I was taught and it's also something I fully believe in ... it's something that I don't really have to work hard to avoid. I don't ever even feel the need to stray away from certain things in my religion, regardless of how many people are doing things around me, because I genuinely believe in those things; so, it's not like I ever feel compelled to stray away from the things that I was taught to believe in.

Farah had participated in several extra-curricular activities including academic clubs as well as running track. "When I ran track, it was like a big thing that I couldn't wear shorts. I was 15 years old, so me having to wear pants made me feel uncomfortable." Farah went to a non-diverse high school and there were no other Muslim girls on the team, "so I had to make those steps myself and was surrounded by people who probably wouldn't get it." While people may not have made Farah feel uncomfortable "just the fact that, first, I have to do this, and then I have to explain myself" at 15 years is a tall ask.

2   Learning from School

Going to a Muslim elementary and middle school allowed her to get a foundational learning of her faith, as well as allowed her to be connected to the community. "I think I'd probably struggle with my Muslim identity a lot more if I didn't go there." The Muslim school also gave her friends that she "latched on to" in high school when she hadn't made any other friends:

> I'd hang out with people in class, but I wouldn't make large enough connections to hang out with them outside of class or actually create that friendship. I remember thinking halfway through high school, I wish I

went to high school without knowing anyone, because I think that would have forced me to make different friends.

Farah shared that the close friends she did end up making were not into partying and were conservative, if non-Muslim, and that made her connection with them comfortable. Her experience in college also centers around the same:

> The biggest thing here is that I don't drink and smoke, right, so that's definitely played a big part in my friendships. It's something I've had to explain here to everyone right off the bat. It's definitely something that I constantly have to talk about, because I think when I first mention that, people thought I was insanely religious and super uptight.

Farah felt herself represented in the curriculum when she took world history. She shared,

> I'd say that was the most accurate because it was taught very objectively. I did have teachers in high school when I was learning US History, who were very obviously racist and maybe didn't like Muslims, so they portrayed it in a very different way, or they'd dance around the issue, or they just wouldn't talk about it, or there'd be like undertones.

Farah couldn't recall ever reading anything in literature in school that represented her but remembered a fictional story she had read about a Muslim American girl that presented her life in a normal and neutral way. Farah was sort of the "voice for Islam" in some of her classes. "Whenever we had a discussion about religion, I'm usually the odd one out because most of my high school was Christian so in world history class, when we were learning about Islam, my friends would ask me to explain certain things."

3   Discussing 9/11

When it came to conversations about 9/11, Farah shared:

> It sometimes comes with an awkwardness. I feel I'm pretty lucky I never had an experience where someone in the classroom feels very opposed to Muslims, where they would say something. Whenever I've been in a classroom, it's always been awkward for everyone, because a lot of times I feel like people don't really know what to say. I don't think I've ever really

been uncomfortable, but I definitely have just naturally felt an awkward-
ness just because I'm thinking 'what are people gonna say?' Are they
going to say anything? How do I respond to that? How do I react to things
like that? But, obviously, I've never been in a position where someone has
said something.

Farah recalled a time when her US History teacher conducted a class on 9/11.
She shared:

I felt that he was Islamophobic, because there was a lot of anger there and
it wasn't directed towards any one of us, but obviously we were Muslim,
so we felt he was dancing around Islam. There was a lot of contempt and
anger there and that's when we started to notice undertones in other
parts of the classes as well.

4   Contemplating Identity

After graduating from her Muslim middle school where there was a religiously
inspired uniform:

I went to high school and, obviously, that was a time for me to explore
how I express myself with clothes and I was, like, very excited. When I
was in ninth grade, I vividly remember having this thought that when
I go to college, 'I'm going to wear whatever I want' in more of a spite-
ful way towards my parents in terms of I'm going to go to college and
they're never going to figure it out and I'm just gonna wear whatever I
want. I remember vividly thinking that. I'm not acting that way now, but
I remember thinking that. Especially in my first semester of high school
that was a huge struggle for me to deal with how I want to wear certain
things. But obviously, I was conflicted because I would never go to school
and change and things like that, because that very much goes against my
moral compass and I'm like a big family person, so I literally would feel so
guilty for my entire life if I did.

Other than clothing, fasting during Ramadan and praying proved to be
challenging in a public high school setting. She recalled not going to prom or
any of the dances at high school because of her Muslim American identity.
Even though her parents had never explicitly said she couldn't go, Farah just
assumed that she couldn't go. These felt like socialization opportunities lost to

Farah. She felt that her high school did not have a big Muslim population, but the school made accommodations when requested. She did not feel that she was treated differently because of her hijab, "but, I think, now, that maybe it's how I present myself. Like, I don't wear a hijab so maybe some people just don't know I'm Muslim." One of her hijabi friends was asked by a substitute teacher "if she knew how to speak English multiple times and it made her feel really uncomfortable because we had been talking, the whole class; it wasn't like she was silent." Farah continued:

> I obviously am a person of color, but I feel more American than a lot of my friends, which is very interesting and I think it's maybe because I did move a lot when I was younger and was constantly making friends and I saw a lot of different places. I think I felt certain pressures just being in certain places where the culture was different and I think that I present myself differently than my friends do just subconsciously weirdly enough. I don't think I'm super outspoken about my religion or culture. If someone asked me, I'm very open, but I'm not the first to walk in and be like, 'Guys, I'm Muslim' and then I explain a ton of things. I kind of just let it flow in terms of like I'm always there to explain things. I will always be true to my Muslim identity and my morals, but I think I present myself as very much American versus Muslim American.

Farah shared that the things that made her Muslim were "definitely how I view the world, I think. Probably the biggest discrepancy between me and my parents has been how I view opportunity." Her parents would always be concerned about security, whereas Farah had no such inhibitions. She felt her parents situated their perceptions of opportunities in relation to the presence of a white mainstream. Farah wondered, "Maybe there's a hierarchy" and perhaps in her father's workplace he felt that pressure:

> But, for me, I grew up here and I don't feel that. I feel like I'm pretty much on par with absolutely everyone, regardless of race, religion, and things like that, and because I grew up around people, and I have the same level education, I have the same experience, why would I ever feel inferior to anyone else. When my parents talk about the stuff that I find pessimistic, I think it's because they came to this country to live and be secure. But for me, I want to go for every opportunity I possibly can, because I feel like I can, because I grew up here, and I was born here, and I feel like I can do everything that everyone around me can. That's probably the most American thing about me, but I think it's also how I act socially. I don't

ever feel I have to only make friends with people of my culture or of my religion.

The climate after any terrorist attack makes Farah very awkward because most people tie these acts to Islam. The Trump election left Farah very shocked and uncomfortable at her high school because:

There were a lot of super conservative people, but there was this one guy who would wear a confederate hat. He had a shirt that had a Lysol spray bottle and it was like spray terrorists or some Islamic undertones; he was very outspoken about it. It felt threatening because what if I ran into him.

MusCrit in Action

The counter-narratives of these 15 Muslim American women share with us telling stories of the lived realities of this particular demographic. The six tenets of MusCrit include: (a) the systemic nature of oppression, (b) the role of identifiability, (c) implications of gender, (d) constructive role of counter-narratives (e) whiteness as property, and (f) essentiality of allies. These six tenets find direct application in an exploration of the counter-narratives shared here.

We can find in these stories the endemic nature of racialized discrimination that exists against this marginalized group. The participants shared at great length the damaging and disparaging stereotypes that exist in popular media and literature. Perceptions of undemocratic tendencies towards prohibitive oppression and terrorism were experienced by several participants. These interviews experienced micro aggressions and outright discrimination in their spaces of learning. Almost all participants shared the discomfort and burden caused by 9/11 in their daily lives. Often they have to explain themselves and apologize on behalf of the entire Muslim world for rogue acts of terrorism. The participants spoke about the social implications that resulted from a hate-induced political climate in the country. The employment of a deficit lens could often be seen when white mainstream engaged with Muslim women.

Identifiability is perhaps the most important and permanent theme that emerges through these counter-narratives. There is a unanimously shared experience by women who could be identified as Muslim as opposed to those who could not. Many times, we heard that when they passed as white or not Muslim, they were treated like the norm, whereas they were working against presumptions if they were easily identifiable. Whether the participants were easily identifiable as Muslim or not, they were all acutely aware of the truth of this experience. This included becoming spokespersons for the entire faith, carrying on their shoulders the burden of explanation and apology and correction. It meant being perceived as a threat or as oppressed. It meant always belonging to some "other" place and not here, it meant being told to "go home." Choosing identifiability therefore, was a choice that required much deliberation from the participants, where they thought about their family, society, and personal commitment before undertaking any action that could be identified as Islamic.

Gender-based stereotypes are prolific when it comes to the experiences of Muslim women. Nearly all participants spoke of cultural norms that existed in this realm, but also of the stereotypes, prejudices, and biases that existed and were fostered by the mainstream. Assumptions of having limited freedoms or not being able to speak English due to lack of access to education were present. Many times, their athletic performance was seen as surprising or that they had supportive fathers was met with disbelief.

Counter-narratives offer us an insight into the lived realities of this demographic, while allowing the population itself to own their story-telling. This renders a truer and more authentic telling which is not hijacked or whitewashed by the mainstream through its lens of white saviorism or cultural deficiency. One particularly recurring moment where this point was nuanced enough to be missed by a white telling and distinct enough to only be captured through an authentic counter-telling was when the participants spoke about their home culture, or ethnicity inspired practices at home and with their families. The participants spoke about the role of parents, grandparents, and other relatives with a warmth and respect-centered acknowledgment while sharing stories of curfews on what time to return home, or opinions on clothing choices etc. The participants understood that the boundaries were not compatible with the mainstream, and would be perceived as limiting of freedom, but they did not feel "trapped" by them. These counter-narratives allow the reader a realignment, a refocus that is centered in the authentic telling of the individuals in question. It offers a dismantling of stereotypes and popular myths that surround the Muslim female experience. It is also these counter-narratives that have helped shape the tenets that we see as part of MusCrit. The process of validation has been cyclical in that sense. A micro-theoretical framework holds no meaning in isolation if it not shaped by that which it seeks to study.

The participants in the study were acutely aware of the cultural deficit lens through which they are seen by the mainstream white. They also recognized the concern that the Muslim elders in the community held about not creating "trouble," but instead working hard towards being successful which was defined by good higher education and a stable career. The participants saw themselves as an extension (or accomplishment) of their parents' American Dream. While this generation is bold in claiming space it understands deeply the reluctance to do so by generations prior.

The participants spoke of the strength afforded to them through allies in a climate of bigotry. The participants felt that they sought spaces with diversity and affinity groups where they could be themselves with ease and not have to explain themselves. One practice that is fast internalized by Muslim women in white spaces is to perform a quick scan or check of what the political views and climate is in a particular space. Whether it is neighborhoods or classrooms, labs or clubs, Muslim women perform an almost automated check to determine if people around them are inclusive or bigoted.

The six tenets of MusCrit as a micro theoretical framework and resultant methodology shape the narratives in a compellingly authentic manner simultaneously placing the stories in the hands of those who own them, while providing the readers a nuanced but deep insight.

Conclusion

The stories of these female Muslim American youth offer us a place to begin. These brave women spoke their truths and shared their experiences of navigating their identities in a place that sees them as others. This telling is an act of social and political assertion; it is a bold conversation on religious identity, even when its perceived as a dirty word, a despised identifier, a demonized and disliked discomfort by whiteness. These stories steer the direction of the dominant discourse which seeks to silence, invalidate, and erase.

By sharing their discomforts, these stories cause you discomfort. By sharing their unapologetic experience of faith, these stories also cause you discomfort. Therein lies the dichotomous experience of being a hyphenated Muslim-American. That is the burden of being. Muslim American youth carry this burden of being on young and tired, yet strong shoulders. They fight battles that were not their making; they represent an entire faith, much larger than themselves in the small daily actions they perform. They do this bravely and timidly all at once. They do it with a simultaneous internalized and externalized self-vision. Standing at the threshold of identity and identifiability is in actuality a daily recommitment to faith and its practice when placed in the scale of acceptable citizenry.

Critical Race Theory has enabled a discourse in education that allows for conversation centered around acknowledgment of oppression and systemic injustice. It allows for crafting unique theoretical spaces that honor and validate the lived experiences of marginalized populations. MusCrit offers us a micro-framing that boldly acknowledges that the Muslim American experience is distinct and therefore requires its own niche. The powerful stories of these 15 participants have helped shape the framing, while also situating us in a meaningful holding space.

References

Abdullah, M. R. (2013). *Islamophobia & Muslims' religious experiences in the Midwest: Proposing critical Muslim theory: A Muslim autoethnography* [Doctoral dissertation]. Kansas State University.

Allen, Q. (2013). "They think minority means lesser than": Black middle-class sons and fathers resisting microaggressions in the school. *Urban Education, 48*(2), 171–197.

Aoki, K., & Johnson, K. R. (2008). An assessment of LatCrit theory ten years after. *Indiana Law Journal, 83*(4), 1151–1195.

Baer, A. L., & Glasgow, J. N. (2010). Negotiating understanding through the young adult literature of Muslim cultures. *Journal of Adolescent & Adult Literacy 54*(1), 23–32.

Bell, D. (1992, September 24). Book discussion on *Faces at the bottom of the well*. http://www.c-spanvideo.org/program/34630-1

Bettez, S. C. (2011). Building critical communities amid the uncertainty of social justice pedagogy in the graduate classroom. *Review of Education, Pedagogy, and Cultural Studies, 33*(1), 76–106.

Bourdieu, P. (1997). The forms of capital. In A. H. Halsey, H. Lauder, P. Brown, & A. Stuart Wells (Eds.), *Education: Culture, economy, and society* (pp. 46–58). Oxford University Press.

Brayboy, B. M. J. (2006). Toward a tribal critical race theory in education. *The Urban Review, 37*(5), 425–446.

Briscoe, F. M. (2005). A question of representation in educational discourse: Multiplicities and intersections of identities and positionalities. *Educational Studies, 38*(1), 23–41.

Caine, V., Estefan, A., & Clandinin, D. J. (2013). A return to methodological commitment: Reflections on narrative inquiry. *Scandanavian Journal of Educational Research, 57*(6), 574–586.

Carr, D. (1986). *Time, narrative, and history*. Indiana University Press.

Chase, S. E. (2011). Narrative inquiry: Still a field in the making. In N. K. Denzin & Y. S. Lincoln (Eds.), *The Sage handbook of qualitative research* (pp. 421–434). Sage Publications.

Clandinin, D. J., & Connelly, F. M. (2000). *Narrative inquiry: Experience and story in qualitative research*. Jossey-Bass Publishers.

Clarke, V., & Watson, D. (2014). Examining whiteness in a children's centre. *Contemporary Issues in Early Childhood, 15*(1), 69–80.

Cole, M., & Maisuria, A. (2007). "Shut the f*** up," "you have no rights here": Critical race theory and racialisation in post-7/7 racist Britain. *Journal for Critical Education Policy Studies, 5*(1).

Cook, D. A., & Dixson, A. D. (2013). Writing critical race theory and method: A composite counterstory on the experiences of black teachers in New Orleans post-Katrina. *International Journal of Qualitatice Studies, 26*(10).

Crenshaw, K. (1991). Mapping the margins: Intersectionality, identity politics, and violence against women of color. *Stanford Law Review, 6*(43), 1241–1299.

Davila, E. R., & Bradley, A. (2010). Examining education for Latinas/os in Chicago: A CRT/LatCrit approach. *Educational Foundations*, 39–58.

DeCuir, J. T., & Dixson, A. D. (2004). So when it comes out, they aren't that surprised that it is there: Using critical race theory as a tool of analysis of race and racism in education. *Educational Researcher, 33*(5), 26–31.

Delgado, R. (1995). *Critical race theory: The cutting edge*. Temple University Press.

Delpit, L., & Kilgour Dowdy, J. (Eds.). (2008). *The skin that we speak: Thoughts on language and culture in the classroom*. The New Press.

Dixon, A. D., Anderson, C. K. R., & Donnor, J. K. (Eds.). (2017). *Critical race theory in education: All God's children got a song*. Routledge.

DuBois, W. E. B. (1903). *The souls of Black folk*. Bantam Books.

Fassin, D. (2011). Policing borders, producing boundaries. The governmentality of immigration in dark times. *Annual Review of Anthropology, 40*, 213–246.

Fatima, S. (2011). Who counts as a Muslim? Identity, multiplicity and politics. *Journal of Muslim Minority Affairs, 31*(3), 339–353. doi:10.1080/13602004.2011.599542

Feagin, J. R., & Feagin, C. B. (1999). *Racial and ethnic relations*. Pearson.

Fernandez, L. (2002). Telling stories about school: Using critical race and Latino critical theories to document Latina/Latino education and resistance. *Qualitative Inquiry, 8*(1), 45–65.

Freire, P. (1973). *Education for critical consciousness*. Continuum.

Garner, S., & Selod, S. (2014). The racialization of Muslims: Empirical studies of Islamophobia. *Critical Sociology, 41*(1).

Gans, H. J. (2016). Racialization and racialization research. *Ethnic and Racial Studies*, 1–14.

Gerhauser, P. T. (2014). Framing Arab-Americans and Muslims in U.S. media. *Sociological Viewpoints, 30*(1), 7–35.

Grosfoguel, R. (1999). Cultural racism and colonial Caribbean migrants in the core zones of the capitalist world economy. *Review, 22*, 409–434.

Harper, S. R. (2013). Am I my brother's teacher? Black undergraduates, racial socialization, and peer pedagogies in predominantly white postsecondary contexts. *Review of Research in Education, 37*(1).

Harris, C. (1995). *Whiteness as property. In critical race theory: The key writings that formed the movement*. The New York Press.

Hernandez, E. (2016). Utilizing critical race theory to examine race/ethnicity, racism, and power in student development theory and research. *Journal of College Student Development, 57*(2), 168–180.

Heschel, S. (2015). The slippery yet tenacious nature of racism: New developments in critical race theory and their implications for the study of religion and ethics. *Journal of the Society of Christian Ethics, 35*(1), 3–27.

Hirsch, E. D. (2006). Why do we have a knowledge deficit? In E. D. Hirsch, *The knowledge deficit: Closing the shocking education gap for American children* (pp. 1–22). Houghton Mifflin.

hooks, b. (1994). *Teaching to transgress: Education as the practice of freedom.* Routledge.

Housee, S. (2012). What's the point? Anti-racism and students' voices against Islamophobia. *Race, Ethnicity & Education, 15*(1), 101–120. doi:10.1080/13613324.2012.638867

Huntington, S. P. (1996). *The clash of civilizations and the remaking of world order.* Simon & Schuster.

Jilani, I. S. (2016). *Muslim American identity under siege: Muslim students' perspectives of American high schools* [Doctoral dissertation]. Northeastern University.

Kolano, L. (2016). Smartness as cultural wealth: An AsianCrit counterstory. *Race Ethnicity and Education, 19*(6), 1149–1163.

Khalifa, M., & Gooden, M. A., (2010). Between resistance and assimilation: A critical examination of American Muslim educational behaviors in public school. *The Journal of Negro Education, 79*(3), 308–439.

Kotchick, B. A., & Forehand, R. (2002). Putting parenting in perspective: A discussion of the contextual factors that shape parenting practices. *Journal of Child and Family Studies, 11*(3), 255–269.

Kress, T. M. (2009). In the shadow of whiteness: (Re)exploring connections between history, enacted culture, and identity in a digital divide initiative. *Cultural Studies of Science Education, 4*(1), 41–49. doi:10.1007/s11422-008-9137-6

Ladson-Billings, G., & Tate, W. F. (1995). Toward a critical race theory of education. *Teachers College Record, 97*(1), 47–68.

Landsman, J. (2001). My white power world. In J. Landsman, *A white teacher talks about race* (pp. 95–102). Scarecrow Press.

Leonardo, Z. (2002). The souls of white folk: Critical pedagogy, whiteness studies, and globalization discourse. *Race Ethnicity and Education, 5*(1), 29–50.

Leonardo, Z. (2013). The story of schooling: Critical race theory and the educational racial contract. *Discourse: Studies in the Cultural Politics of Education, 34*(4), 599–610.

Lynn, M., & Dixson, A. D. (2013). *Handbook of critical race theory in education.* Routledge.

Miles, R. (1989). *Racism.* Routledge.

Misawa, M. (2012). Social justice narrative inquiry: A queer crit perspective. *Adult Education Research Conference.*

Museus, S. D. (2013). *An Asian critical theory (Asian Crit) framework* (pp. 18–29). Indiana University Bloomington.

Naji Amrani, I. (2017). *Racialization: The experiences of Muslim graduate students in higher education after September 11* (10265001) [Doctoral dissertation, Northeastern University]. ProQuest Dissertations & Theses Global.

Olneck, M. (2000). Can multicultural education change what counts as cultural capital? *American Educational Research Journal, 37*(2), 317–348.

Omi, M., & Winant, H. (1994). *Racial formation in the United States from the 1960s to the 1990s.* Routledge.

Omi, M., & Winant, H. (2014). *Racial formation in the United States.* Routledge.

Ortiz, L., & Jani, J. (2010). Critical race theory: A transformational model for teaching pedagogy. *Journal of Social Work Education, 46*(2), 175–93.

Pager, D. (2006). The dynamics of discrimination. *National Poverty Center: Working Paper Series, 6*(11), 1–47.

Petro, A. M. (2017). *Studying religion in the era of Trump.* Religion & Culture Forum, Boston University.

Ponterotto, J. G. (2005). Qualitative research in counseling psychology: A primer in research paradigms and philosophy of science. *Journal of Counseling Psychology, 52*(2), 126–136.

Ramsay, N. J. (2014). Intersectionality: A model for addressing the complexity of oppression and privilege. *Pastoral Psychology, 63*(4), 453–469.

Reid, A. (2014). *Native American identity formation in relation to educational experiences.* Social Studies Capstone Projects.

Reissman, C. K. (2008). *Narrative methods for the human sciences.* Sage Publications.

Said, E. D. (2008). *Orientalism.* Vintage.

Sirin, S. R., & Fine, M. (2008). *Muslim American youth: Understanding hyphenated identities through multiple methods.* New York University Press.

Solórzano, D. G. (1998). Critical race theory, race and gender microaggressions, and the experience of Chicana and Chicano scholars. *International Journal of Qualitative Studies in Education, 11*(1), 121–136.

Solórzano, D. G., & Yosso, T. J. (2001). From racial stereotyping and deficit discourse toward a critical race theory in teacher education. *Multicultural Education, 9*(1), 2–8.

Solórzano, D. G., & Yosso, T. J. (2002). Critical race methodology: Counter-storytelling as an analytical framework for education research. *Qualitative Inquiry, 8*(23), 23–44.

Solórzano, D. G., & Yosso, T. J. (2009). Critical race methodology: Counter storytelling as an analytical framework for educational research. In E. Taylor, D. Gillborn, & G. Ladson-Billings (Eds.), *Foundations of critical race theory in education* (pp. 131–147). Routledge.

Sue, D. W. (2010). *Microaggressions and marginality: Manifestation, dynamics, and impact.* John Wiley & Sons.

Thomas, J. M. (2010). The racial formation of medieval Jews: a challenge to the field. *Ethnic & Racial Studies, 33*(10), 1737–1755.

Tindongan, C. W. (2011). Negotiating Muslim youth identity in a post-9/11 world. *High School Journal, 95*(1), 72–87.

Writer, J. H. (2008). Unmasking, exposing, and confronting: critical race theory, tribal critical race theory and multicultural education. *International Journal of Multicultural Education, 10*(2), 1–15.

Writer, J. H. (2013). Native resistance through art: A contestation of history through dialogue, representation, and action. *International Journal of Education & the Arts, 14*(SI 2.4).

Yosso, T. J. (2005). Whose culture has capital? A critical race theory discussion of community cultural wealth. *Race, Ethnicity and Education, 8*(1), 69–91.

Index